CU00793917

SLEEP STORIES FOR KIDS

A COLLECTION OF TALES WITH DRAGONS, UNICORNS, DINOSAURS, AND ALIENS.

© Copyright 2021   All rights reserved.

This document is geared towards providing exact and reliable information with regards to the topic and issue covered. The publication is sold with the idea that the publisher is not required to render accounting, officially permitted, or otherwise, qualified services. If advice is necessary, legal or professional, a practiced individual in the profession should be ordered.

- From a Declaration of Principles which was accepted and approved equally by a Committee of the American Bar Association and a Committee of Publishers and Associations.

In no way is it legal to reproduce, duplicate, or transmit any part of this document in either electronic means or in printed format. Recording of this publication is strictly prohibited and any storage of this document is not allowed unless with written permission from the publisher. All rights reserved.

The information provided herein is stated to be truthful and consistent, in that any liability, in terms of inattention or otherwise, by any usage or abuse of any policies, processes, or directions contained within is the solitary and utter responsibility of the recipient reader. Under no circumstances will any legal responsibility or blame be held against the publisher for any reparation, damages, or monetary loss due to the information herein, either directly or indirectly.

Respective authors own all copyrights not held by the publisher.

The information herein is offered for informational purposes solely, and is universal as so. The presentation of the information is without contract or any type of guarantee assurance.
The trademarks that are used are without any consent, and the publication of the trademark is without permission or backing by the trademark owner. All trademarks and brands within this book are for clarifying purposes only and are the owned by the owners themselves, not affiliated with this document

Table of contents

INTRODUCTION TO SLEEPLESSNESS IN CHILDREN

Sleeplessness can likewise be called insomnia and can be characterized as trouble starting sleep (considered in children as trouble in nodding off without a parental figure's mediation); looking after sleep (visit arousals during the night and trouble coming back to sleep without a guardian's intercession), or getting up sooner than the standard timetable with failure to come back to sleep—insomnia influences around 30% of children in their initial two years[3]. After the third year of life, the commonness stays stable at around 15%. This issue, when incessant, can have consequences for psychological advancement, mindset guideline, consideration, conduct, and personal satisfaction, of the youngster as well as the whole family.

We, as a whole, realize that great sleep propensities are significant for children. In any case, guardians' bustling work routines, after-school exercises, and schoolwork would all be able to cut into family time on weeknights and can bigly affect how a lot of a youngster sleeps.

Given the way that time together for such a significant number of family units begins at around 6 or 7 o'clock or considerably later at night on a weeknight. Furthermore, since specialists state young children generally need around 9 to 11 hours of sleep—which implies they have to hit the sack around 8 or 9 o'clock, contingent upon what time they have to find a workable pace—allow for anything other than supper, schoolwork and perusing one short book section together.

However, it tends to be especially significant for grade-schoolers to get enough shut-eye. How much a youngster sleeps can bigly affect her development and advancement.

Most guardians picture a crying child when they consider kids and sleep issues. Numerous more established kids and teenagers have issues sleeping as well, including inconvenience resting and awakening much of the time in the night.

Sadly, not getting a decent night's sleep can influence your youngster's state of mind and conduct during the day, prompting school and order issues.

Insomnia

Like grown-ups, children with insomnia either experience difficulty resting, staying unconscious, or are basically not very much rested after what ought to be a typical measure of time sleeping. Notwithstanding being sleepy during the day, the side effects of youth insomnia can include:

- Irritability

- Mood swings

- Hyperactivity

- Depressed mind-set

- Aggressiveness

- A diminished capacity to focus

- Memory issues

Reasons for Childhood Insomnia

One regular explanation that numerous children don't get enough sleep is that they hit the sack past the point of no return. This is frequently on the grounds that guardians have unreasonable desires for how a lot of sleep their kids need or in light of the fact that their kids are over-planned and are taking part in an excessive number of exercises or have an excessive amount of schoolwork. Or on the other hand, your youngster may just be up late messaging, chatting on the telephone, playing computer games, or sitting in front of the TV.

Recall that children between the ages of 6 and 12 need around 10 to 11 hours of sleep every night, and adolescents need around 9 hours of sleep every night.

On the off chance that you set a reasonable bedtime, and your youngster is still not getting a decent night's sleep, the basic reasons for insomnia can include:

• Poor sleep propensities

• Caffeine

• Stress

• Obstructive sleep apnea (wheezing)

• Side impacts of medications, including energizers used to treat ADHD, antidepressants, corticosteroids, and anticonvulsants

• Asthma (hacking)

• Eczema (tingling)

• Depression

• Anxiety

• Restless legs disorder

• The neurodevelopmental issue, for example, chemical imbalance, mental hindrance, and Asperger's disorder.

Medicines for Childhood Insomnia

In spite of the fact that guardians regularly need to go to a solution to treat their kid's insomnia, it is considerably more imperative to search for any fundamental clinical or mental issues that may be dealt with first.

For instance, if your youngster has obstructive sleep apnea and wheezes boisterously around evening time and habitually quits breathing, at that point, he may need to have his tonsils and adenoids evacuated. Or then again, if your kid has a continuous nighttime hack since his asthma is ineffectively controlled, at that point, he may require more grounded deterrent asthma medication. On the off chance that your kid has sleep apnea, asthma, or is discouraged, at that point, a sleeping pill isn't the appropriate response.

Likewise, the sleeping pills that we as a whole observe advertised on TVs, for example, Ambien CR and Lunesta, have not been affirmed for use in children. Medications which are sometimes utilized when fundamental and proper to include:

- Sedating antidepressants, including amitriptyline, and Remeron

- Melatonin

- Clonidine, particularly if your youngster likewise has ADHD or conduct issues.

- Risperdal, particularly if your youngster likewise has a chemical imbalance or conduct issues.

- Antihistamines, despite the fact that these generally cause daytime tiredness and would simply be utilized for an exceptionally brief period.

Except if there is another or co-sullen analysis as a reason for your kid's insomnia, a remedy is normally not the appropriate response.

Non-Drug Treatments for Primary Childhood Insomnia

Non-tranquilize medications for essential insomnia, or youth insomnia that isn't brought about by another ailment, can include:

• Restricting time spent in bed to just sleeping, which implies no perusing, doing schoolwork, or sitting in front of the TV in bed.

• Having an exceptionally steady calendar of when your kid hits the hay and awakens, including ends of the week and occasions

• Teaching your youngster about unwinding methods, including diaphragmatic breathing, dynamic muscle unwinding, and visual symbolism, which he can utilize when he is resting

• Stopping animating exercises 30 to an hour prior to bedtime, for example, playing computer games, staring at the TV, messaging or chatting on the telephone

• Getting up and accomplishing something calm, for example, perusing, if your youngster doesn't nod off inside 10 to 20 minutes

• Avoiding caffeine

• Exercising routinely

General Tips to Help The Kids Develop Better Sleep Habits

Attempt these tips to enable your youngster to grow great sleep propensities and sleep well each night.

Adhere to daily practice. A decent bedtime routine is basic with regards to ingraining great sleep propensities in kids. A shower, nightgown, brushing teeth, and a couple of pages from a book—whatever your nighttime custom is, make certain to adhere to it reliably so your kid comprehends what's in store and can without much of stretch travel through each routine productively every night.

Bedtime Routines To Help Children Fast Sleep

Breaking point electronic energizers. Try not to let your kid utilize the PC, check her telephone, or stare at the TV, in any event, an hour prior to bedtime. These electronic screen exercises can be invigorating and can meddle with falling and staying unconscious.

Keep her room agreeable for sleeping. Ensure your youngster's room isn't excessively hot, excessively stuffy, or excessively brilliant. (In the event that your youngster fears the dull, pick a night light that will keep her room as diminish as could be allowed.) Bedrooms that hush up, dim and cool are ideal for a decent night's rest.

Put in a safe spot additional time for getting up to speed. On the off chance that your evaluation schooler has more youthful or more seasoned kin, be certain you give every youngster singular time with each parent. (To spare time, you can turn off with your accomplice and exchange father and mother time every night.)

Control tricky caffeine. You wouldn't let your evaluation schooler down some espresso before bed. Be that as it may, caffeine can likewise prowl in nourishments and beverages you may not presume, for example, chocolate, packaged tea, and even some non-cola soft drinks. Watch for nourishments that contain caffeine, and if your youngster requests dessert, stick to sound organic product when it's near bedtime.

Watch your youngster rather than the clock. How much your kid needs to sleep can shift contingent upon his individual needs. A few kids may do fine and dandy on 8 hours of sleep, while others need a strong at least 10. Search for indications of sleep hardship, for example, hyperactivity, cantankerousness, and memory or focus issues. On the off chance that you see these signs, get your youngster to bed early, find a way to expel battles about bedtime, and be predictable about bedtime schedules each night.

Kid Bedtime Routines Dos and Don'ts

Regardless of whether you have a baby, little child, kindergartner, or preteen, pragmatic order methodologies and a decent bedtime routine can be the distinction between great sleep propensities and a ton of sleepless evenings.

And keeping in mind that any of the books can assist you with showing signs of improvement, despite the fact that they all utilization various techniques, it is critical to see that the vast majority of these child-rearing specialists stress the key of having a decent bedtime routine for a decent night's sleep.

Bedtime Routines for kids

A bedtime routine incorporates everything that you do with your infant or more seasoned kid not long previously, and up to the time that you put him to sleep, for example, cleaning up, they keep going diaper change, putting on night robe, saying petitions, and perusing a bedtime story, and so forth.

The objective of a decent bedtime routine is for your kid to nod off all alone, without being shaken, staring at the TV, or with you resting alongside him. Along these lines, in the event that he wakes up later, he ought to have the option to comfort himself and fall back asleep without requiring any additional assistance. Then again, in the event that he connects nodding off with being shaken, for instance, on the off chance that he does later wake up in the center of the night, he likely won't have the option to return to sleep except if you rock him back to sleep.

Kids Bedtime Routines Dos and Don'ts

There is no outright right approach to set up a bedtime schedule. A few kids like to hear a bedtime story, others might need to discuss their day, and some may simply need to state their supplications and rest. For whatever length of time that your kid nods off effectively and sleeps throughout the night, at that point, your bedtime routine is likely functioning admirably.

Different things that you should probably do as a feature of a decent bedtime routine can incorporate that you:

• Do start early. It is a lot simpler to start a decent bedtime routine when your child is youthful than to attempt to change poor sleep schedules when you have a little child or preschooler who, despite everything, isn't sleeping great.

• Do make your bedtime routine age-proper. Your kid's bedtime routine will change after some time. For instance, while it is normal for an infant or more youthful newborn child to nod off nursing or to drink a jug of a recipe, you can attempt to begin putting your infant down while he is languid yet at the same time wakeful once he is four or five months old.

• Do keep your bedtime routine genuinely short. A decent bedtime routine will presumably last around 10 to 15 minutes, or somewhat more in the event that you incorporate a shower.

• To utilize a security object as a piece of your bedtime schedule. A security object, similar to a soft toy or cover, can be a significant piece of a decent bedtime schedule, particularly for little children and preschoolers. These sorts of things generally aren't sheltered in the lodging for more youthful newborn children, however.

• Do be steady in your bedtime schedule. Your bedtime routine may change after some time, as your youngster gets more seasoned. However, it ought to be genuinely steady from every day, beginning simultaneously and going in a similar request. For instance, a little child's bedtime routine may begin at 8 p.m. also, incorporate a shower, putting on nightwear, perusing a couple of bedtime stories, getting in bed, and the last goodnight.

• Do offer a few decisions in your bedtime schedule. Your youngster can't pick when to hit the hay. However, you can let him have some force in his bedtime routine by letting him have a decision over which night robe to wear and which books to peruse, and so on.

• Do comprehend that a bit of crying can be alright. A few kids, regardless of what you do. This can be alright on the off chance that they rapidly settle down, and you are open to let them weep for a couple of moments. Remember that even the Ferber Method doesn't advocate just letting kids cry throughout the night.

• To utilize a night light. Hardly any kids like to sleep in obscurity, which makes a night light valuable.

• Do remember dental cleanliness for your bedtime schedule. Regardless of whether you are cleaning your infant's gums or reminding your more seasoned youngster to brush and floss his teeth, legitimate dental cleanliness is a decent propensity that you can remember for your kid's bedtime schedule every night.

• Do remind your kids to utilize the restroom one final time before hitting the sack. This is particularly significant for more youthful kids who, despite everything, have issues with bedwetting.

Much the same as there is plenty of right approaches to have a decent bedtime schedule, there are some incorrect ways and things you ought to keep away from.

• Don't haul out your bedtime schedule. If you are not cautious, your kid will haul out your bedtime routine any longer with rehashed calls for beverages, snacks, or to utilize the washroom. Attempt to adhere to your unique bedtime, however.

• Avoid invigorating exercises not long before your bedtime schedule. Particularly if your youngster experiences difficulty nodding off, you ought to normally quit invigorating exercises 30 to an hour prior to bedtime, for example, playing computer games, sitting in front of the TV, or chatting on the telephone.

• Avoid caffeine before bed. Remember that notwithstanding pop and tea; caffeine can be a shrouded fixing in different nourishments, including espresso enhanced frozen yogurt and chocolate, and so on.

• Avoid poor sleep affiliations. This incorporates things like scouring your kid's back until he nods off, having music playing, or keeping the TV on since if your youngster figures out how to connect nodding off with something to that effect, he will require help in the event that he later awakens. What's more, no, essentially keeping the TV or music on throughout the night doesn't work. If your kid awakens, he will, in any case, shout out for you and need your assistance to return to sleep.

•   Don't accept that your youngster will just exceed poor sleep propensities. Sadly, if nothing is done, numerous children who have sleep issues as newborn children and babies keep on sleeping inadequately even once they start school. The sooner you fix your youngster's poor sleep propensities, including beginning a decent bedtime schedule, the better.

A COLLECTION OF DINOSAURS BEDTIME STORIES FOR KIDS

THE DINOSAURS CAMP

Sometime in the distant past, there were four dinosaur companions who wanted to do everything together. They made fortresses, they swam in waterways, and they played tag. However, one thing they had never done was go outdoors.

One day Stegs chose to change that, so he said to his dinosaur companions: "We have to go outdoors under the stars. We can have a fire and eat wieners."

"I love eating hounds," Terry stated, however, no one listened on the grounds that Terry consistently discussed eating hounds. The remainder of the companions just gestured in understanding.

So the following day, they pressed their tent and strolled to a close-by backwoods. They set up their tent on a level spot of grass around of pine trees.

"The branches are high to such an extent that we can absolutely cook sausages securely," Bron said to his companions.

"I love eating hounds," Terry said.

The remainder of the companions assembled wood and set up the tent. At that point, they strolled for 10 minutes and found a rivulet where they played catch and swam on their backs. Bron, Stegs, and Tri ate the plants from the base of the freshwater stream.

"Would we be able to eat hounds now?" Terry inquired. Also, the time had come to return to the tent since it was getting dull, and they were in a new spot, at the point when they kicked back, they off a fire.

"Terry, don't contact the wieners," Bron said. "We will do the cooking." And cook they did. They cooked 20 bundles of sausages over the fire.

"We each have four bundles to eat," Stegs clarified.

"Would I be able to have 20?" Terry inquired.

"No!" They all replied.

So they each had four bundles as they discussed how much enjoyment it was to camp. Following an hour of eating, it was Tri's chance to pose an inquiry.

"Where is the restroom? We did all eat four bundles of wieners, and I can't be the one in particular who needs to utilize one."

By the looks on his companions' faces, he was not alone.
"I don't accept we brought one," Bron conceded. "I don't figure it would have fit in the tent regardless of whether we'd have brought one."

At that point, apparently all of a sudden, a young lady showed up.

"Greetings dinosaurs, my name is Leah, and I know where there is a potty you can pee on."

"I'm sorry, Leah, we have to do the other thing," Terry said.

"This is a potty you can pee and crap on. Tail me. It's up a lot of blue advances."

All the dinosaurs, aside from Stegs who expected to watch the fire, followed Leah. It wasn't some time before they found the blue advances that prompted what Leah continued calling the Pee Fort. They all alternated, and even Stegs got a go-to go. At that point, they returned to their pit fire and bid farewell to Leah, being certain to say thanks to her for the Pee Fort.

"That is the last time we go outdoors without pressing our potty," Tri reported before finding a good pace to bed.

"I love eating hounds," Terry said on a signal.

"We know. Goodbye."

THE LAST DINOSAURS

In a lost place that is known for tropical timberlands, on the main mountain in the district, caught inside an old volcanic pit framework, experienced the last ever gathering of huge, fierce dinosaurs.

For a great many years, they had endured all the progressions on Earth, and now, driven by the incomparable Ferocitaurus, they were wanting to leave covering up and to overwhelm the world again.

Ferocitaurus was a magnificent Tyrannosaurus Rex who had chosen they had invested an excessive amount of energy confined from the remainder of the world. Thus, over a couple of years, the dinosaurs cooperated, obliterating the dividers of the incredible hole. At the point when the work was done, all the dinosaurs deliberately honed their paws and teeth, in preparation to threaten the world indeed.
Altogether different from what they had
been utilized
 inside the hole. In any case, for a considerable length of time, the dinosaurs progressed forward, steadfast.

At last, from the highest point of certain mountains, they saw a community. Its homes and townsfolk appeared modest spots. Never having seen people, the dinosaurs jumped down the mountainside, prepared to wreck whatever hindered them...

Nonetheless, as they moved toward that little town, the houses were getting greater and greater... what's more, when the dinosaurs, at last, showed up, it worked out that the houses were a lot greater than the dinosaurs themselves. A kid who was passing by stated: "Daddy! Daddy! I've discovered some small dinosaurs! Would I be able to keep them?"

Also, that is the way things are. The unnerving Ferocitaurus and his companions wound up as pets for the town children. Perceiving how a huge number of long periods of advancement had transformed their species into diminutive person dinosaurs, they discovered that nothing kept going forever and that you should consistently be prepared to adjust.

DINOSAURS IN MY BED

Richy lay shuddering in his bed. The sky was bursting at the seams with blasting sounds and splendid flashes simply outside his window.

Fifteen minutes prior, he asked, "Mother, will the tempest keep going long?"

"Kindly, don't stress," she said. "The meteorologist guaranteed it would disregard Truro rapidly. Presently get some sleep."

But it didn't, and he proved unable.

Richy tuned in to his morning timer. "Tick… Tick… Tock." The night appeared to go on for eternity. Seconds transformed into minutes.

At that point, into what appeared hours.

Over the house, uproarious lightning crashes made him duck further under the covers. Outside thunder even shook his window.
He was a major kid now. What's more, he must be courageous. Father even helped him plan for this awful climate.

Just in the event that it endured throughout the night.

Presently his knapsack was covered up under the covers. It was loaded up with most loved toys, games, and comic books. Indeed "Panda" bear he had since the age of two.

Mother ensured Richy likewise had a couple of treats. A tremendous pack of popcorn was near his correct side. What's more, a pack of undulated chips was on the other.

His family had gone rising in Cape Breton, a weekend ago. So he was presently a kid with outdoor understanding. What's more, he realized that how would generally be valiant.

What was moving around his toes? "Ouch, that hurt," his trembling voice, murmured. The commotion outside was so noisy Richy could barely think.

Through the window, a dim sky shut out the stars.

The kid was out of nowhere apprehensive. What was under the cover? He was interested and scrounged through his knapsack.

"OMIGOSH," Richy said. "I overlooked my electric lamp."

He slid up and flung himself over the floor. Richy chased around until he discovered it in the top bureau compartment.

Rapidly bouncing go into bed, he constrained cold feet down to the end. Uncovered toes laid on something unpleasant and sharp. Presently it was by all accounts slithering around his lower legs.

Yowser! He wasn't the only one in bed!

He checked under the spreads where it was dark as coal, practically like being outside. Rather than sparkling stars lit up, spots looked progressively like eyes.

Thundering originated from behind his left leg.

Richy bit to his left side thumb and turned on the electric lamp. "That alarming sound couldn't be… ?" he faltered.

Truly, a dinosaur! Be that as it may, that was unthinkable, right? Dinosaurs couldn't fit under bed blankets, having a place with a young man, living inside his home. Isn't that so?

Wrong. Gazing back at him was a Stegosaurus. What's more, it tasted his Hostess vinegar chips, the one little sack with a couple of pieces left.

"Escape, you!" Richy roared, attempting to be bold. The animal thundered something back under the sweeping sky and rushed into a shadowy corner.

New clamors got the kid's consideration. His electric lamp helped select moving shadows. What was happening? He pondered. There was a Triceratops and a Deinonychus.

Also, a Tyrannosaurus!

"Run!" Richy shouted. Out of nowhere, he had a feeling that he was the just a single alive on the planet. In any case, he was still under his cover that appeared to extend out there and even high above him.

He searched for someplace to cover up.

Cold feet could scarcely move. It resembled an alternate world under the covers. His heart walked to the beat of a drum. Lightning zipped, then destroyed under his sweeping sky.

Enormous animals started to pursue littler ones.

Hustling toward him was a Dicraeosaurus. This was a quiet plant-eater and would not hurt him. However, Richy couldn't take any risks.

He pulled a fire motor from his rucksack. Bouncing into the front seat, Richy turned the alarm on full speed. Everything it did was harmed his ears.

A Ceratosaurus and Albertosaurus limited after him. They resembled enormous amicable mutts needing to play. Be that as it may, Richy didn't wish to get squashed.

He hurried up pedal. Furthermore, the firing motor jumped forward.
Before long, the street turned into a tight way, pointing straight for the woodland. Richy immediately stopped. At that point, he bound on new tennis shoes from his rucksack.

He likewise brought his whistle. Abrasive blowing cautioned everything to escape his direction. A whirlwind of feet got away down the path, each progression beating hard.

One arm held firmly to 'Panda.'

The breeze passed over his top, sending it into the separation. Branches grabbed at his face. He would not like to get squashed or eaten by those dinosaurs.

The tempest outside was nothing contrasted with wild animals pursuing him under his cover. How did the entirety of this occur in any case?

Snarls and speeding feet kept pace behind him. Venturing into his knapsack, Richy grabbed his in-line skates. Presently, he figured, it ought to be anything but difficult to skate away securely.

That is until a subtle tree root sent him carelessly into the mud.

Presently it was pick up the pace time to climb a tree.

"Mother, where are you?" Richy yelled. "Daddy!" Skinny legs mixed up the storage compartment. What's more, similar to a monkey climbed higher from branch to branch.

Out of nowhere between two appendages was the leader of a Brontosaurus. It grinned as it bit a significant piece of leaves. "What's your concern?" it appeared to state.

"Richy! RICHYWW!" somebody called. Voices appeared to move to and fro and around like echoes. Truly, individuals were yelling his name!

The kid hurriedly lost his covers, sat up, and gazed at mother and father. He squinted as morning's sun looked between Venetian blinds.

"Panda" was as yet tucked safely under his arm.

"I see you discovered our amazements under your covers," mother said.

Richy took a gander at his mother.

"You know. Recall the dinosaur models you requested a week ago?"

"What's more, I'm pleased with you," father said. "Look how perfectly you stacked them on your bureau."

Richy felt abnormal, as father pointed.

In a flawless line was a motorcade of beautiful dinosaurs. They were following an amicable Dicraeosaurus, with a fierce-looking Tyrannosaurus Rex toward the stopping point.

Driving the entire gathering was a figure of a young man.

Furthermore, he was holding firmly to a teddy bear.

THE MAGIC PAINTBRUSH

A FIVE DAY BEDTIME STORIES SERIES

Didier and Francis find that their paintbrushes are enchantment and make their photos genuine.

NIGHT DAY ONE

Some time ago, there was an attractive kid called Didier. He was four years of age. He wanted to take a gander at dinosaurs in his dinosaur book, and envision what it resembled to draw a genuine dinosaur… from life!

At some point, he was sitting in his bedroom with his paint and paintbrushes and an excellent image of a dinosaur. It was a Triceratops, which implied that it had three major horns originating from its temple. Its face looked ravenous, similar to it might want to eat a young man, or maybe only a major bowl of porridge.

Didier took his red paint and made the dinosaur the shade of a fire motor. He utilized green paint for the horns. At that point, since despite everything looked hungry, he painted a major bowl of porridge directly close to it.

He was respecting how well he had shaded in the dinosaur. There were not really any spots whatsoever where he had gone outside the lines. Yet, at that point – what was this? He saw a modest minimal purple spot toward the side of his image. God, help us! He was more likely than not going outside the lines, all things considered!

He didn't stop to imagine that the little dab was purple, and he had just utilized red and green paints (which, as we probably are aware, together with don't make purple by any stretch of the imagination!). He simply put down his paintbrush, and with his little finger, rubbed the paper tenderly, to check whether the spot would fall off.

OWWW! The page was spiky!

He pulled his finger back and saw somewhat sore on his pinky finger. There was even a touch of blood close to his fingernail. He figured he would need to put a staying mortar on it.

He sucked his finger until it felt much improved and took a gander at the image. Did he envision it? Or then again had the dinosaur moved, only a small tad?
Sufficiently sure, the paper didn't feel like paper when he contacted it. Rather, it was unpleasant and layered, similar to a snake, or maybe like a scab.

He ran his finger tenderly down where the dinosaur's spikes made a fence along his spine. That piece of the image was pointy.

He heard a minor ROAR! Like the sound of somebody's TV on an alternate floor. Might it be able to have been his dinosaur? He didn't set out touch the mouth…

At that point, the dinosaur made another ROAR, and there was no uncertainty about it this time. Out of nowhere, the bowl of porridge that he had made for his dinosaur vanished. It appeared that the dinosaur had gobbled everything up.

NIGHT DAY TWO

There was no uncertainty that Didier had painted himself a genuine live dinosaur. It never appeared to move. However, it was eager, Didier could tell. He could guess by the flickering little eye that appeared to take a gander at him as he got his paintbrush again.

On the off chance that the dinosaur was eager, at that point, Didier would need to paint him some more nourishment. In any case, what might a dinosaur want to eat?

He, however, that a few desserts may be yummy. He painted flawless pink chocolate with a little heart on it and some jam snakes. He viewed the dinosaur picture cautiously. Sufficiently sure, very soon, the desserts and the chocolate that he had drawn adjacent to the dinosaur just – vanished. It resembled he had never painted them.

Didier put his face near check whether the photos he'd painted had left any follows, as sometimes happens when you utilize an eraser to wipe out your drawing that you did unintentionally. Yet, there was not a hint of the desserts and chocolate he had painted, or of the porridge. There was only one – marginally less eager looking, and still extremely sharp, Triceratops.

Exactly at that point, Didier's older sibling Francis strolled into the room.

"What's happening with you?" said Francis.

"I don't have the foggiest idea… " said Didier, attempting to consider something that wasn't valid. He would not like to disclose to Francis directly as of now that he had a genuine live composition of a dinosaur eating porridge and desserts.

Francis inclined down and took a gander at the dinosaur.

"That is a really decent dinosaur Didier," he said. "Be that as it may, I figure you've done his head somewhat off-base."

What's more, before Didier could state anything by any stretch of the imagination, Francis had gotten a paintbrush and, utilizing orange paint, was beginning to paint on the Triceratops' head.

"NO!" shouted Didier. "Try not to do that!" But it was TOO LATE!

Francis gave a shout as the finish of his paintbrush was snapped directly off by a lot of furious Triceratops teeth.

"What befell my paintbrush?" cried Francis.

"The dinosaur is alive!" said Didier. "I painted him quite recently, and when I had got done with painting him in, I think I spiked my finger on him! He's extremely sharp! What's more, he's eager. He's as of now eaten one major bowl of porridge, a chocolate with a heart in the center, and some jam snakes."

"Amazing!" said Francis, his eyes shining. "I can't trust you painted a genuine Triceratops! How could you do that? Is it true that you are enchantment?"

"I don't have the foggiest idea!" said Didier. "I simply utilized these paintbrushes here."

Francis grabbed the paintbrushes from his younger sibling and spread them the whole way across the work area. They made a wreck. Each shading you could envision was in their fibers. At that point, he grabbed a bit of paper and began to paint.

"What are you painting?" said Didier.

"I'm painting a tiger!" said Francis. "See it? It has large orange ears, and dark stripes this way."

He painted the tiger and a decent tiger; it was as well. Similar to it was going to swat someone. He shaded it cautiously then remained back to see his work. Sufficiently sure, he'd made a fine showing. He hadn't gone outside the lines by any stretch of the imagination—all with the exception of a minor purple speck toward the side of the tiger's tail. Francis grimaced. He didn't care about going outside the lines.

"What's this?" he said. He took his finger and cautiously rubbed at the little purple spot. "OWWWWWWWWW!" he said. "It bit me!"

"The tiger bit you?"

"It bit me! Look! I have a sore, directly here. On my pinky finger."

"It's simply equivalent to me," said Didier. "My triceratops did the very same thing when I contacted it. Maybe the tiger doesn't care for you contacting his tail. Why do whatever it takes not to deliberately give him a pat?"

Francis was somewhat stressed over this thought since he previously had an irritated finger. In any case, cautiously, inch by inch, centimeter by centimeter, he put his finger towards the tiger picture.

What do you think it felt like? It felt like the gentlest butterfly you've at any point contacted. It felt like a modest, sparkling bugs web floating from the entryway.

"It's lovely!" said Francis in stunningness.

"It must be the paintbrushes," said Didier. "I think we have enchantment paintbrushes. All that we paint transforms into something genuine. I think Francis, you would do well to paint something for the tiger to eat, in light of the fact that he is presumably ravenous."

"Be that as it may, what do tigers eat?" said Francis.

"I don't have a clue," said Didier.

"I think they eat gazelles," said Francis. "I don't know whether I realize how to draw a pronghorn."

"You could attempt," said Didier. "It's somewhat similar to a pony, yet with wavy horns on its head."

"Alright," said Francis. So cautiously, he dunked his paintbrush into some flawless yellow paint, and alongside the tiger, he painted an extremely pleasant looking eland. It wound up with delightful eyelashes, a long neck, and a little grin at the side of its mouth.

At the point when he had wrapped up the impala, he was content with it. He figured it must be a young lady gazelle since she was so lovely.

In any case, he had overlooked while he was drawing, the motivation behind why he was drawing a gazelle.

"Gee golly," said Didier, acknowledging what Francis, in the fervor of painting a lovely animal, had overlooked. "Gracious, the poor impala! She will be eaten by that tiger! What will we do?"

There wasn't a lot of time. The tiger appeared to swivel its ravenous little eye towards the pretty eland.

"Possibly, you might you be able to simply put a major squiggle of white paint on her! Wipe her out!" said Didier. "Rapidly, before the tiger eats her."

"Be that as it may, if I do that, she will even now vanish!" said Francis. "That will be only the equivalent, won't it? On the off chance that I wipe her out, I won't have the option to paint her once more. I may paint an alternate impala, yet she wouldn't be the very same one. That would be much the same as in the event that a dinosaur ate me, and afterward Mum and Dad thought, well it's alright, we've despite everything got Didier. He's a young man as well."

"You're correct. That wouldn't be the equivalent by any stretch of the imagination," said Didier.

The two of them thought exceptionally hard. They didn't know whether they envisioned it, yet the gazelle appeared to look somewhat frightened. What might they be able to do?

"Rapidly! What animal eats tigers?" said Francis to Didier.

"I don't have the foggiest idea!" shouted Didier.

"Be that as it may, possibly…," Francis stated. At that point, they took a gander at one another and thought of something. They said together: "Dinosaurs!"

"In any case, how might I get my dinosaur onto your image?" asked Didier.

"Goodness, it's awful, you proved unable," said Francis. "It would need to be an alternate one. However, take a gander at my image. There's no room on it for another dinosaur. No room at all for any large animals. See, here's the tiger, and here's the gazelle, and there's no more space for another huge animal."

"Goodness," said Didier. At that point, he had another thought. "Why not eat the tiger, Francis?" he inquired.

"What do you mean?" Francis answered, thinking Didier had gone somewhat senseless.

"All things considered, I've seen individuals eating paper previously, you know when they unintentionally chomp a cupcake wrapper or even a sweet wrapper. It doesn't taste really awful, you know. It's the only sort of like eating nothing. So perhaps you could do it. Simply eat the tiger, and disregard the pretty gazelle."

"He may just be paper," said Francis. "Yet, that tiger despite everything bit me previously. What might occur if I put him in my mouth, and he scratched my gums? Imagine a scenario where he kicked and made one of my teeth drop out.

Didier shrugged. "That wouldn't be so awful," he said. "Your tooth is as of now somewhat unstable, right?"

Yet, Francis' eyes looked exceptionally enormous and adjust, similar to supper plates, and he didn't generally appear to need to place the tiger in his mouth.

"Might you be able to paint an alternate sort of nourishment?" said Didier, considering something other than what's expected, on the grounds that he truly would not like to make Francis have a sore in his mouth. "Shouldn't something be said about desserts? Or on the other hand porridge? My triceratops loved that!"

Francis deliberately painted a major bowl of porridge, much the same as Didier's, with the exception of this time he shrouded it in strawberries and chocolate sauce. He figured a tiger would not have the option to oppose a major bowl of porridge, particularly when it was secured with strawberries and chocolate sauce.

In any case, when he had painted it, the bowl stayed precisely where it was. Didier put out a finger and felt it – maybe it was cold? Yet, no, it was steaming and warm and comfortable like the most pleasant sweet you've at any point eaten on a virus winter's day. It was incomprehensible that a tiger who preferred porridge dislike this bowl of porridge.

The tiger's little beady eyes appeared to swivel. They appeared to swivel toward the pretty pronghorn. "I don't think he prefers porridge… " said Didier with fear.

"I have it!" yelled Francis! The yell was uproarious to such an extent that the tiger, the triceratops, and even the pronghorn appeared to surprise. The bowl of porridge even appeared to wobble in its bowl, that is the manner by which noisy Francis' cry was, and that is the means by which great his thought truly was.

"What?" said Didier. They were using up all available time, and they knew it.

"No time to clarify!" said Francis. He plunged his paintbrush into the closest shading – darker – and before Didier could even ask one sentence more, Francis had painted an extraordinary enormous enclosure around the tiger. He immediately put in the bars, and in the nick of time!

The tiger squinted, and the littlest little bit of the impala's foot vanished. Be that as it may, it was just a touch of the foot and no more. The pronghorn herself looked pitiful, yet Francis immediately painted another foot right where hers had vanished, and her grin appeared to return. The foot was somewhat extraordinary to how it had been previously, however without a doubt, that was superior to being the tiger's supper.

Didier has Francis an embrace. He was so upbeat for the impala.
"Speedy, paint some more nourishment for him. He doesn't care for porridge. However, perhaps you could paint him some sushi. Everyone likes sushi. What's more, it's pretty much nothing, so you can fit it here, toward the side of his confine."

Francis thought it was a smart thought. So he painted some yummy sushi, and the tiger should truly have been exceptionally ravenous, in light of the fact that before they knew it, the sushi had vanished. Francis needed to paint another six sushi before the tiger was fulfilled.

So now the young men were left with a triceratops, a pronghorn, and a tiger in an enclosure to take care of. It appeared they ought to be cautious before they painted whatever else. As of now, they needed to go through ten minutes painting some pleasant green grass for the impala, and afterward painting some decent dishes of water for every one of them to wash their meals down. At that point, they needed to paint an evening time sky, since they figured the animals must get worn out at this point. At that point, they needed to paint cushions, quilts, a bed, and at that point, the entire picture on the two bits of paper was getting very swarmed.

"It's late young men!" said a voice, and Mummy strolled in. She took a gander at the photos. "Stunning! They're extremely extraordinary pictures!" she said. "State, Daddy, come view these photos the young men have painted!"

Daddy came in and took a gander at them. His grin was colossal, in light of the fact that he thought they were so acceptable. "I'd prefer to put them on the ice chest," he said.

"You can't do that!" said Francis and Didier rapidly. "We don't need them on the cooler. We need them in our bedroom."

"In your bedroom!" shouted Mummy. "Where will you put them? All the dividers are shrouded in your photos as of now. There's no more space. No, no, these photos are unique. See what you've finished with the tiger's hide! What's more, the confinement! Furthermore, that sushi looks so genuine, and I could nearly contact it!" Mummy put out her hand to contact the sushi, yet in the nick of time, Francis whisked the paper away from her. Fortunately, in light of the fact that he realized that the tiger's teeth were extremely sharp.

"Gracious," said Mummy, baffled.

"We just truly like these photos," said Didier. "Is that alright?"

"Obviously it's alright," said Mummy and Daddy, and they gave the young men a kiss and left the room.

"Thank heavens. That was close," said Francis. "We can't inform Mummy and Daddy concerning the paintbrushes. Imagine a scenario where they thought they were excessively risky. No, we have to keep them
someplace safe. How about we get them all now, and put them at the base of the toy box. Nobody will discover them there."

So they got all the paintbrushes and cleaned up the paints and put them at the base of their toybox. They, however, would be sheltered there. In any case, how wrong they were!

A COLLECTION OF PRINCE AND PRINCESS BEDTIME STORIES FOR KIDS

THE PRINCE CALLED THOMAS

There was previously an extremely uncalled for Prince, in spite of the fact that he appeared the ideal Prince: attractive, courageous, and astute. Prince Thomas gave the feeling that nobody had ever disclosed to him the idea of equity. In the event that two individuals came to him over some contest, anticipating that he should resolve the issue, he would rule for whichever one appeared to be generally enchanting, or generally attractive, or whoever had the most attractive sword.

Tired of this, Thomas' dad, the King, chose to get an astute man to show his child equity. "My shrewd companion, it would be ideal if you remove him," said the King, "and don't bring him back until he's prepared to be an equitable and reasonable King."

The savvy man left by pontoon with the Prince, however, they endured a wreck and wound up together, as the main survivors, on a desert island. There they had no nourishment or water.

For the initial not many days, Prince Thomas, an incredible tracker, figured out how to get some fish. When the savvy old man requested that he share the fish with him, the youthful Prince cannot. In any case, occasionally later, the Prince's angling turned out to be less effective, while the elderly person was figuring out how to get feathered creatures consistently. Similarly, as the Prince had done, the astute man wouldn't share his catch. Thomas got more slender and more slender, until he at last burst into tears and asked the insightful man to share a portion of his nourishment to spare him from starving to death.

"I will just impart them to you," said the astute man, "on the off chance that you give me you've taken in your exercise." The Prince, having realized what the shrewd man was attempting to show him, stated, "Equity comprises of sharing what we have, similarly."

The astute man saluted him and gave him some nourishment.

That equivalent evening a boat protected them from the island. On their arrival venture, they halted some time by a mountain, where a man perceived the Prince, and let him know: "I am Max, head of the Maximum clan. It would be ideal if you help us, we are experiencing difficulty with the neighboring clan: the Minimums. We both offer meat and vegetables, and we contend about how to share them out."

"Easily settled," addressed the Prince, "Check what number of you there are altogether, and share the nourishment in equivalent extents."

Thus, he had just utilized what the savvy man had instructed him.

In any case, in the wake of saying this, came the sound of thousands of cries from the mountainside.

A crowd of irate men came running over and drove by the boss, who had posed the inquiry, they jumped on Prince Thomas, and took him, prisoner.

Thomas couldn't comprehend this by any stretch of the imagination. They tossed him in a jail cell, and let him know, "You attempted to execute our kin. If you don't tackle this issue by dawn tomorrow, you will remain in jail until the end of time."

They had done this to the Prince in light of the fact that the Minimums were little and various, though the Maximums were gigantic. However, there were not many of them.

So the arrangement proposed by the Prince would have starved the Maximums to death.

The Prince comprehended the circumstance and went through all that late evening reasoning.

The following morning, when they approached him for an answer, he stated: "Don't share the nourishment similarly. Rather, share it out as indicated by how a lot of every individual eats. Give individuals nourishment as indicated by their size."

The Maximums loved this answer such a lot of that they discharged the Prince, held an extraordinary gathering, garlanded him with gold and gems, and offer him and the shrewd man a protected excursion.

As they were strolling along, the Prince remarked, "I've gained some new useful knowledge. It isn't reasonable to forgive the equivalent to all. The reasonable thing is to share, yet you should consider individuals' contrasting needs."

The astute man grinned with fulfillment.

Effectively near the palace, they halted in a little town. A man of exceptionally poor appearance got them and ensured they were very much joined in. In the interim, another man, of poor comparative appearance, tossed himself to the ground before them, asking. A third, who appeared to be a rich man, sent two of his hirelings to watch out for the Prince and the astute man and gave them what they required. The Prince so making the most of his time there that, on his takeoff, he gave the locals all the gold which the Maximums had given him. Hearing this, the poor man, the bum, and the rich man, all approached the Prince, everyone requesting his offer." How will you share it out?" asked the savvy man, "the three are altogether different, and it would appear that the person who parts with increasingly gold is the rich man..."

The Prince dithered. The savvy man was correct. The rich man needed to pay his hirelings, he was the person who had burned through generally gold, and he had taken care of them well.

In any case, the Prince was beginning to build up a feeling of equity, and something disclosed to him that his first decision on this issue was not adequate.

At long last, the Prince took his gold and made three heaps: one major, another medium measured, and the last one little. In a specific order, he offered them to the poor man, the rich man, and the homeless person. Saying his farewells, the Prince set off with the insightful man, making a beeline for the palace.

They strolled peacefully, and when they arrived at the palace door, the insightful man asked: "Reveal to me something, youthful Prince. I'm not catching justice's meaning to you?"

"I think equity lies in sharing, considering necessities, yet additionally the benefits of the person."

"Is that why you gave the littlest heap to the troublemaking poor person?" asked the shrewd man, happily.

"Indeed, that is the reason. I gave the large heap to the poor man who took care of us so well. In him, I saw both need and legitimacy, since he helped all of us he could, in spite of being poor. The medium heap was for the rich man. Despite the fact that he took care of us superbly, he truly didn't have a lot of requirements for increasingly gold. The little heap I provided for the irksome poor person since he didn't do anything deserving of remuneration. Notwithstanding, given his extraordinary need, it was likewise optioned to give hive something to live on." clarified the Prince.

"I think you'll be a fine King, Prince Thomas," finished up the astute man, grasping the Prince.

Also, he was correct. From that point on, the Prince got known all through the realm for his reasonableness and intelligence. A few years after the fact, his rising to the position of authority was praised by all. Thus it was, that King Thomas became recognized as the best chief the realm had ever had.

INVITATION TO THE BALL

There was a horribly messy Prince who constantly overlooked his folks when they requested that he clear up his wreckage. The neighboring realm's Princess - who he was covertly enamored with - sorted out an extravagant ball, and welcomed all the Princes from close by lands. The messy Prince was energized and set himself up with extraordinary consideration.

Upon the arrival of the ball, his room was muddled to the point that he was unable to discover his greeting. He searched urgently, yet it was no place to be seen. So he chose to clean up his entire room. Luckily he discovered his greeting on the table.

Be that as it may, when he at long last showed up at the ball, he was late and everybody had left.

The Prince was distressed and had most unquestionably taken in his exercise.

In any case, not all things are misfortune.

The Princess had not discovered a sweetheart at the party, and sometime later, she set up another gathering. This time, since he had everything efficient, the Prince didn't lose his greeting. He found a good pace on time and met the Princess, who fell head over heels in adoration with him.

THE BOY WHO NEARLY TURNED INTO A PRINCE

A King who had no children declared a challenge to conclude who might be made a Prince and beneficiary to the position of authority. The kid who finished all the assessments, albeit magnificent, was eager, and that stressed the King. So the King chose to test the kid, taking him to the woodland with a pooch, and guiding him toward an extraordinary fortune in the focal point of the forested areas.

The King left the kid with the canine, saying that if upon his arrival, the kid and the fortunes were still there, sitting tight for him, at that point, the kid would get the Kingdom. The kid acknowledged the demand, however soon, he became anxious, and in spite of the pooch's admonitions, the kid went into the woods. When he did as such, the fortune vanished.

Thus, the kid lost both the fortune and the opportunity to acquire the Kingdom.

WORKS OF THE KINGDOM

Some time ago, a King requested his two children to manufacture two enormous reservoir conduits to supply water to his nation domains, which were in an extremely poor state because of an extraordinary dry spell. The principal child removes a portion of his dad's wealth and part of the military. With them, he voyaged north, where he requested the individuals of those terrains to buckle down on building the water channel. He directed the work cautiously, paying the residents reasonably, and completing the undertaking inside the anticipated two years. Pleased with his work, he came back to the palace, just to discover the spot amidst festivities for the coming delegated of his sibling as King. He was informed that his sibling had taken just a single year to manufacture his water system in the south and that he had figured out how to carry out the responsibility with scarcely any troopers or cash.

This appeared to be so abnormal to the primary sibling that he started to explore the southern water channel. What he discovered added up to in excess of a couple of abnormalities. He came back to the palace, advising his dad to keep away from this franticness of making his sibling King.
"You realize the amount I love my sibling. However, he probably has gone insane. He has hauled our great name through the drain. He fabricated his water passage veering off from the plans. He made such a significant number of outlets that scarcely a large portion of the water shows up at the imperial domains. He went up against the head administrator before the locals, and he left without paying any of the laborers. He even utilized your warriors as workers. What's more, who knows? Possibly that is just the start..."

The King, looking lovingly at his child, answered.

"My child, what you state is valid. Your sibling had the activity to alter the water channel to improve it, the knowledge to propose something which would improve the lives of everybody. Thus he persuaded the locals to work rapidly and without pay. He had the mental fortitude to go up against the head administrator to safeguard equity, and the magnetism to set his fighters to work a bigger number of hours than the residents considerably. His responsibility was extraordinary to such an extent that he himself was the person who worked hardest on the venture, overlooking his Princely status. You know what, my child? This is the reason everybody loves your sibling and would do anything he was to ask of them. He is more than their King. He is their pioneer".

The Prince left, somewhere down in thought. He came to perceive that the expressions of his dad for sure highlighted the enormity of his sibling. What's more, decisively, he raced to his sibling, to compliment him.

THE RESPECTFUL PRINCE AND THE DWARVES

Sometime in the distant past, the King's two Princes were playing in a woods, and - meeting each in turn - they ran over four dwarves who requested that they be increasingly cautious.

The diminutive primary person had a migraine, and he asked them not to yell. The subsequent smaller person was painting a scene, and he requested that the children move away on the grounds that they were shutting out the light. The third midget was doing a goliath jigsaw puzzle in the street, and he asked the children not to step on it. The fourth diminutive person was watching a butterfly, and he asked them not to alarm it away.

The Prince who regarded others did as the dwarves asked. However, the impolite Prince overlooked the dwarves' requests and continued annoying them. At night, the two young men had gotten isolated and lost. They expected to return to the palace rapidly.

Every one of them independently went over the four dwarves once more and requested their assistance.

The other Prince showed up a lot later and was rebuffed for it. He currently comprehended that it's greatly improved to regard everybody in the event that you need to have companions.

THE SEVEN CAPTIVE PRINCESSES

At the point when the malicious Witch of the Summits detained the seven Princesses in the seven castles of the seven mountains, watched by seven birds of prey, seven monsters, and seven mythical beasts, nobody figured they could ever return alive. The daring Sir Mariels joined a veteran band of respectable knights to ride to the Great Summits, rout the birds of prey, beasts, and mythical beasts, and free the Princesses.

The knights entered each castle to protect the youngsters. These spots were so cold and dim that the Princesses looked practically dead. The bold knights thought about what sort of awful fiendishness there must be in the witch's dark heart to have detained the Princesses there. At the point when freed, the little youngsters were massively appreciative to their rescuers, since life in those phones was the emptiest, and most exhausting one would ever envision. Grinning, they tuned in to the knights to relate their deeds, and they became hopelessly enamored with their boldness and dauntlessness.

Be that as it may, on showing up at the last castle, which appeared to be no unique from the others, they found a lovely inside, brilliantly enlivened and kept up, loaded up with light and shading. One could even hear wonderful mood melodies as if this was some supernatural spot. Also, when they hurried to protect the seventh Princess from her niche in the most noteworthy pinnacle, as they had finished with the others, they didn't discover her there. They searched wherever for her until, following the mysterious music, they wound up in a little parlor. They found no enchantment there, yet sat in the room was a blissful Princess dexterously playing the harp.

Nothing vexed the knights more than the little youngster's glad and eager demeanor. She was refined, shrewd, rich, and had an exceptional present for human expressions. In contrast to different Princesses, in whom the impact of their detainment was effectively obvious, the last Princess appeared to have carried on a considerably more dynamic and fascinating life. Yet, after much addressing and request, the knights could just presume that she had been similarly detained and single as the others.

Shocked, they searched the palace, searching for clarification, until they showed up at the library. Numerous books were missing, and at exactly that point did they understand the explanation: the entire of the remainder of the castle was brimming with books. On each table and the household item, you could without much of a stretch discover a book or some likeness thereof. The Princess had read constantly!

Thus it was that she had figured out how to learn and live such a large number of encounters that it appeared, to her, that she had never been detained. She had experienced her detainment occupied with such a significant number of exercises that she had not even once been exhausted.

The arrival venture was surely a bizarre one. The Princesses – separated from the last one – ended up being so exhausting and uninteresting that none of the knights had the option to restore their adoration. Despite what might be expected, all the knights were taken by the youthful Clara, who, not being diverted by the knights' deeds or the glimmer of their shield, had the option to pick her genuine affection at her recreation, a lot later on.

THE LAKE PRINCESSES

There were two wonderful Princesses who, when still youthful, had been seized by an unfriendly King. The King organized to have them taken to an overlooked lake where they were relinquished on a little island. Here they were to stay forever, monitored by a frightening lake beast.

Just when the devilish King and his court of wizards and psychics had been ousted, did it become realized that a courageous Prince was bound to free the Princesses from their bondage.

At the point when the breeze conveyed this news to the island, it filled the Princesses' lives with trust. The most youthful, who was a lot better and more excellent than her sister, calmly sat tight for her adoration, making little designs from blossoms and dirt, and singing affection melodies. The more established Princess, be that as it may, didn't appreciate pausing.

- "I'll need to plan something to help the Prince salvage me. At any rate, so he knows where I am, or he comprehends what the lake beast resembles."

Resolved to support the Prince, she set to work, making signal fires, building towers, burrowing burrows, and a thousand different things. In any case, the awful lake beast consistently gave a valiant effort to scupper her arrangements.

As time went on, the more established sister felt progressively awkward. She realized the Prince would pick the more youthful sister, so she felt there wasn't a lot of sense in continuing pausing.

Starting there on, she focused on attempting to escape from the island and the lake beast, not agonizing in any way, shape, or form over the Prince or whether he would save them.

Each morning she would set up an alternative departure plan. However, the beast would consistently figure out how to demolish it. The getaway endeavors went on for a long time and constantly finished with the beast catching her. They became like a round of feline and mouse between the Princess and her watchman. Each getaway endeavor was more unique and astute than its ancestor, and each type of disclosure was perpetually unobtrusive and astounding. They put such a lot of exertion and creative mind into their arrangements that toward the finish of every day, the Princess and the beast would go through hours talking like companions about how they had each readied their technique. What's more, when the moon turned out, they would state goodbye until tomorrow, and the beast would plunge down to the watery profundities.

At some point, the beast says goodbye to the Princess like this:

- "Tomorrow, I will permit you to go. You are a cunning and bold little youngster. You don't have the right to stay detained this way."

In any case, the next morning, the Princess didn't attempt to getaway. She sat by the water, holding up until the beast showed up.

- "For what reason haven't you gone?"

Asked the beast.

- "I would not like to disregard you here all. The facts demonstrate that you're unnerving, and you're gigantic, yet you also are shrewd, and you merit an option that is superior to simply guarding Princesses. Why not accompany me?"

- "I can't,"

addressed the beast, unfortunately

- "I can't leave the island, and I'm joined to it by a long chain. You should leave all alone."

The Princess moved toward the startling monster and embraced it energetically. So firmly did she embrace the beast that is separated into a thousand pieces? What's more, out from among those pieces seemed a thin, grinning youngster, with a similar smart articulation as had the lake beast.

Thus it was that the Princesses found their saving Prince and that he had been with them from the beginning. They hadn't realized that for him to save them, first they would need to save him. This was just made conceivable gratitude to the soul and uplifting mentality of the more seasoned sister.

Furthermore, the Prince, being the shrewd youngster he was, was in question about which Princess he would decide to wed... leaving the more youthful sister to her melodies, her excellence, and

her sweetness,.. ever sitting tight for some silly Prince that would adore a young lady with such minimal activity.
£
The Respectful Prince and the Dwarves

Sometime in the distant past, the King's two Princes were playing in a woodland, and - meeting each in turn - they went over four dwarves who requested that they be progressively cautious.

The diminutive primary person had a migraine, and he asked them not to yell. The subsequent smaller person was painting a scene, and he requested that the children move away on the grounds that they were shutting out the light. The third smaller person was doing a goliath jigsaw puzzle in the street, and he asked the children not to step on it. The fourth smaller person was watching a butterfly, and he asked them not to startle it away.

The Prince who regarded others did as the dwarves asked, yet the insolent Prince disregarded the dwarves' supplications and continued troubling them. At night, the two young men had gotten isolated and lost. They expected to return to the palace rapidly.

Every one of them independently ran over the four dwarves once more and requested their assistance.

The other Prince showed up a lot later and was rebuffed for it. He presently comprehended that it's vastly improved to regard everybody in the event that you need to have companions.

THE RUNAWAY PALACE

Long, sometime in the past, when the world was so loaded with the enchantment that even the littlest stone could hold a thousand privileged insights, there was a palace that was alive. Since it rested constantly, no one knew its mystery. It remained that route until the Princess who lived there wedded a Prince who was a bold and solid warrior, however, had such an awful temper, that even the littlest bother would make him throw things around and pummel entryways and windows. After his last triumph, he let the sort and sweet Princess leave the palace to travel and arrange the harmony, disregarding the Prince to live for quite a while.

The Prince's weariness made his awful temper deteriorate, and, with the spending days, an ever-increasing number of imprints and scratches showed up on the dividers and floors of the palace, which became grimy and ignored. At some point, when the Prince went out, the palace - irritated at how it was being dealt with - woke up and moved without precedent for some years. It chose to hole up behind a slope yet was huge to the point that it didn't take long for the Prince to discover it once more.

The palace attempted to get away from ordinarily, yet the Prince would consistently discover it effectively and afterward release his anger, causing increasingly more harm. One night, having become burnt out on the Prince's activities, the palace bolted every one of its entryways and windows while the Prince rested. It ran for quite a long time and days, disregarding the harm and decimation the Prince was causing while caught inside. At the point when the palace at long last halted and opened its entryways, the Prince found that they were encompassed by ice and day off, the middle of the appalling virus.

"The North Pole? How would I leave?" pondered the Prince as he investigated his new environment.

Subsequent to searching throughout the morning and discovering nothing, the Prince chose to return to the palace to heat up. Be that as it may, when he attempted to open the entryway, he discovered it bolted. He hit into the entryway irately; however, all he figured out how to do was annihilate his close, solidified hands. Sooner or later, the entryway opened marginally, and the Prince ran towards it, just for it to close forcefully.

"Moronic palace! It appears to be irate with me!"

The palace was, in fact, irate with the Prince and shook every one of its windows to tell him.

"With the goal, that's the manner in which you need it?" yelled the Prince. "All things considered, prepare, if this is war. Also, I have never lost a fight."

The Prince and the palace had the most bizarre battle possible. While the Prince attempted to get in by breaking the windows, the palace did whatever it could to keep him out. In that insane war, the virus started to freeze the Prince's feet and break the palace dividers. At the point when he was totally ice cold all the way through, the Prince - victor of a thousand fights - understood that the best way to win this one is to make harmony. Thus the Prince started to fix the palace and to control his annoyance and wrath so as not to harm it once more. The palace before long understood that it loved the fixes significantly more than the inept battling and that solitary that brutish Prince could do them. Before sufficiently long, the palace opened its ways to permit the Prince to shield from the cold around evening time, and clean and fix by day.

Causing him a deep sense of shock, the Prince found that he truly delighted in doing the fixes, and quickly the palace looked sublime by and by. To such an extent, that one night it at long last pardoned the Prince, shut its entryways, and ran right back to its nation.

They showed up not long before the Princess, who was charmed with the condition of the palace and the improved character of her better half, presently scarcely intrigued by wars and battling anymore. The enduring harmony and the Prince's fixes implied the palace could come at last resume its quiet sleep.

The main thing anybody thinks about this one of a kind palace is that it was brought down stone by stone and conveyed far and wide. A portion of the stones could well be a piece of your home today, so don't let your indignation and temper cause it any harm...

A COLLECTION OF CASTLE AND EMPIRES BEDTIME STORIES FOR KIDS

EDWARD AND THE DRAGON

Edward was the most youthful knight in the realm. He was still basically a kid, however, was so fearless and keen that, without battling anybody by any stretch of the imagination, he had vanquished every one of his adversaries.

At some point, while riding through the mountains, he ran over a little cavern. On entering it, he discovered it was gigantic, and that inside was a noteworthy castle, so large that he figured the mountain couldn't be genuine, and that is more likely than not been an exterior put there to shroud the castle.

On approaching the castle, Edward heard the sound of voices. Without faltering, he climbed over the castle dividers and followed the voices.

"Anyone here?" he inquired.

"Help! Help us!" came the reaction from inside, "we've been secured here for a considerable length of time, serving the mythical castle beast."

"Winged serpent?" thought Edward, not long before a gigantic flying fire nearly consumed him alive. Edward spun quietly around, and tending to the horrible mythical serpent up close and personal, stated: "It's okay, Dragon. I excuse you for what you simply did. You likely didn't have any acquaintance with it was me."
The mythical serpent was exceptionally astounded at words like these. He never anticipated that anybody should face him and positively, not in such a shameless way.

"Plan to battle, predominate! I don't give a fig what your identity is!" thundered the winged serpent.

"Hold up a minute. Indeed, unmistakably you don't have the foggiest idea who I am. I am the watchman of the Great Crystal Sword!" proceeded with Edward, who - before battling - was fit for making a wide range of things up. "You surely understand that the sword has slaughtered many monstrosities and winged serpents and that in the event that I unsheathe it, it will fly straight into your neck and execute you."

The mythical serpent had never known about such a sword. However, this startled him. He unquestionably didn't care for the sound of something cutting his throat. Edward continued talking.

"Regardless, I need to allow you to battle me. We should make a trip to the opposite side of the world. Over yonder, there's a snow-shrouded mountain, and at the summit, there's an extraordinary pinnacle. At the highest point of the pinnacle, there's a brilliant enclosure where a wizard made this sword. There the sword loses all its capacity. I'll be there, yet I will just hang tight for you for five days."

On saying that, Edward raised a dust storm and vanished. The mythical beast thought Edward had played out an enchantment, yet he had just covered up in certain shrubberies. Needing to battle with that impudent knight, the mythical beast immediately flew out of the cavern, towards the opposite side of the world, in an excursion which endured over a month.

At the point when Edward was certain the winged serpent was far away, he left his concealing spot, entered the castle, and set free all the detainees inside. Some had been absent for a long time, and when they got back, everybody commended Edward's extraordinary knowledge.

Also, shouldn't something be said about the mythical beast? All things considered, would you be able to accept that on the opposite side of the world, there was actually a frigid mountain with a major pinnacle on top, and a gold confines in addition?

Well truly, the monster crashed into the pen and couldn't get out; and there he remains, trusting that somebody clever will one day come and salvage him...

THE MOST PROMINENT WARRIOR

Mikel was a fearless youngster, a specialist swordsman, and he longed for turning into the best warrior on the planet. In the entire armed force, there was certifiably not a solitary trooper who could beat him. He wanted to become the leader of the military one day, so he could supplant the fearful old General who was at present in control. The King enjoyed Mikel, yet when Mikel educated him regarding his desire to be designated, the King looked somewhat stunned and stated,

"Your craving is true. However, I'm apprehensive it can't occur at the present time. You, despite everything, have a lot to learn."

That was the most exceedingly awful thing that could have happened to Mikel, who turned out to be angry to such an extent that he raged out of the palace, resolved to gain proficiency with all there was to think about battling wars. He went to a wide range of schools and universities, improving his system and his quality, however without truly learning any new insider facts, until one day he went to an extremely uncommon school, an immense dark stronghold on an incredible mountain. On his way, he discovered that the old General had examined there, and Mikel continued, always resolved to be acknowledged into the school to become familiar with the incredible privileged insights of war. Prior to entering the post, he was made to deliver every one of his weapons.

"You won't need those anymore. Here you'll be showing signs of improvement ones", said the gatekeeper. Mikel was intrigued, and he gave his weapons to a little dark man who promptly tossed them into a pit. One of the educators, a genuine elderly person of barely any words, went with Mikel to his room.

As he left, the elderly person stated, "In a hundred days, the preparation will begin." A hundred days! From the start, Mikel thought this was a joke, yet he before long understood the man had been not kidding. The main days were loaded up with anxious strain, and Mikel attempted all way of senseless strategies to attempt to get them to begin the preparation. It didn't work, however, and he wound up standing by calmly, appreciating every day as it might have been.

On the hundred and the first day, the main exercise started. "You have just figured out how to utilize your principle weapon: persistence," started the savvy old instructor. Mikel could scarcely trust it, and he let out a concise laugh. The elderly person proceeded to help him to remember all the insane tricks Mikel had pulled in the principal days when he had been overwhelmed by restlessness. Mikel needed to concede the instructor was correct.

That sounded great to Mikel, that is, until he got himself attached hand and foot to a seat; a seat is remaining on a little platform, and with many residents scaling to attempt to give him a decent whack. He had a brief period to act, and the ropes were tight; he was unable to escape this one. At the point when the residents climbed on the platform, they set to work, giving him a decent beating.

Exactly the same exercise was rehashed for a considerable length of time, and Mikel realized he would need to attempt some new strategies. He attempted and bombed ordinarily until it occurred to him that the best way to forestall the assault is to manage the residents' resentment. In the next days, he continued conversing with them, until he figured out how to persuade them that he was no danger to them, yet rather a companion. At last, he was convincing to such an extent that they surrendered their threatening vibe without anyone else, and such a kinship created, that they offered to vindicate Mikel by turning on the instructor. It was day 200 and two.

"You, as of now, control the most impressive weapon - the weapon of words. That which you couldn't accomplish with quality or sword, you dealt with your tongue," said the elderly person.

Mikel concurred, and he arranged to proceed with his preparation. "Presently, this is the most significant piece of all. Here you will confront different understudies", said the educator. He went with Mikel to a corridor where seven different warriors were pausing. All of them looked solid, bold, and furious, similarly as Mikel did. That, yet in everyone, you could recognize traces of the knowledge picked up in the initial two exercises. "Here you will battle, each man for himself. The victor will be the sole survivor," said the educator.

Thus, every morning, the seven warriors would battle it out. Every one incapacitated, every one astute, they required the gathering of residents, and the warriors set about attempting to impact the locals against their adversaries, utilizing just words and tolerance. Every one formulated stunts and misdirections to assault the others when they least anticipated it, and without to such an extent as pointing a blow themselves, they are prevailing with regards to coordinating a brutal fight. In any case, as the days passed, Mikel understood that the two his own quality, and his townspeople, were debilitating. So he changed his strategies.

Utilizing his endowment of the talk, Mikel surrendered the battle, and he proposed utilizing his residents to enable the others to recoup. His rivals were thankful to have one less enemy, as well as the welcome idea of help, and they escalated their battling. In the interim, an ever-increasing number of residents started to join Mikel's gathering, until at long last, one of the seven, named Thunder, figured out how to triumph over the others. Next to Thunder, there now stayed just a couple of residents. At the point when Thunder had completed the battle and appeared to be successful, the educator stepped in, saying, "No, just one can see at present stay standing." Thunder sent Mikel an undermining look. However, Mikel ventured forward and stated,
"You truly need to battle? Wouldn't you be able to see there are fifty times a greater amount of us? These men quit any pretense of everything for me, I have let them live unreservedly, and in harmony, you must choose between limited options."

On hearing this, the couple of townspeople left next to Thunder moved over and joined Mikel. He had won!

The elderly person at that point entered, smiling from ear to ear. "Of all the extraordinary weapons, harmony is my top choice. At some point or another, everybody joins the side of harmony," he said. Mikel grinned. Genuinely, in that school, he had figured out how to employ significantly more remarkable weapons than those he had submitted at the entryway. Days after the fact, Mikel said his farewells, offering gratitude to the elderly person. He came back to the palace, arranged to request a pardon from the King for his rashness. At the point when the King saw him approach modestly, with neither shield nor weapons, he gave Mikel an astute and knowing grin.

SEVEN CAPTIVE PRINCESSES

At the point when the underhanded Witch of the Summits detained the seven Princesses in the seven castles of the seven mountains, watched by seven birds of prey, seven monsters, and seven winged serpents, nobody figured they could ever return alive. The daring Sir Mariel's joined a veteran band of respectable knights to ride to the Great Summits, rout the hawks, monsters, and mythical beasts, and free the Princesses.

The knights entered each castle to save the youngsters. These spots were so cold and dull that the Princesses looked practically dead. The valiant knights thought about what sort of horrible underhandedness there must be in the witch's dark heart to have detained the Princesses there. At the point when freed, the little youngsters were hugely appreciative of their rescuers, since life in those phones was the emptiest, and most exhausting one would ever envision. Grinning, they tuned in to the knights to relate their deeds, and they experienced passionate feelings for their fortitude and courage.

In any case, on showing up at the last castle, which appeared to be no unique from the others, they found an excellent inside, magnificently embellished and kept up, loaded up with light and shading. One could even hear wonderful ambient melodies, just as this was some mystical spot. What's more, when they raced to safeguard the seventh Princess from her anteroom in the most elevated pinnacle, as they had finished with the others, they didn't discover her there. They searched wherever for her until, following the supernatural music, they wound up in a little family room. They found no enchantment there, however, sat in the room was an upbeat Princess capably playing the harp.

Nothing unsettled the knights more than the little youngster's upbeat and excited disposition. She was refined, cunning, exquisite, and had an exceptional present for expressions of the human experience. In contrast to different Princesses, in whom the impact of their detainment was effectively unmistakable, the last Princess appeared to have carried on a significantly more dynamic and intriguing life. Yet, after much addressing and request, the knights could just reason that she had been similarly detained and lone as the others.

Astonished, they searched the palace, searching for clarification, until they showed up at the library. Numerous books were missing, and at exactly that point did they understand the explanation: the entire of the remainder of the castle was brimming with books. On each table and the household item, you could without much of a stretch discover a book or some likeness thereof. The Princess had read constantly!

Thus it was that she had figured out how to learn and live such a large number of encounters that it appeared, to her, that she had never been detained. She had experienced her imprisonment occupied with such huge numbers of exercises that she had not even once been exhausted.

The arrival venture was absolutely an odd one. The Princesses – separated from the last one – ended up being so exhausting and uninteresting that none of the knights had the option to restore their adoration. In actuality, all the knights were extremely taken by the youthful Clara, who, not being diverted by the knights' deeds or the glimmer of their reinforcement, had the option to pick her genuine affection, at her relaxation, a lot later on.

EXTRAORDINARY PALACE OF FALSEHOODS

Sometime in the distant past, all the spirits set about structure two palaces; a palace of truth, and a palace of falsehoods. Each time a kid came clean, a block was made for the palace of truth. The spirits of truth would then take it and add it to the developing dividers.

In simply a similar way was the palace of falsehoods manufactured. Every block was made when a kid lied. The two palaces were amazing - the best on the planet - and each gathering of spirits endeavored to attempt to ensure that their own palace was the best. To such an extent that the lying spirits, who were substantially more precarious and beguiling, sent a gathering of spirits to the world to get children to lie. These spirits were effective and began getting a lot more blocks. Subsequently, their palace increased and progressively terrific.

In any case, at some point, something weird occurred in the palace of falsehoods. One of the blocks transformed into a cardboard box. A little later, another block transformed into the sand, and afterward, another transformed into glass, and crushed. Thus, gradually, it turned out to be certain that at whatever point a falsehood was found, the block that it had made changed its structure, was squashed, lastly vanished. Right now, the palace of falsehoods got more fragile and more vulnerable, and at last, it totally self-destructed.

At this, everybody, including the lying spirits, comprehended that you couldn't utilize lies for anything. They are never what they have all the earmarks of being. Thus no one can tell what they will transform into.

THE BRAVE BOY AND THE MULTICOLORED GHOST

Quite a long time ago, a kid went on his days off to an extraordinary castle. He went through all the rooms and halls, aside from one wing, which he never entered inspired by a paranoid fear of the haziness there.

In that piece of the castle carried on a startled kaleidoscopic phantom. He had never left that zone since he feared the light.

Both the kid and the phantom attempted to defeat their dread a few times, however, without progress. That was, until one day when the kid called up the entirety of his mental fortitude and began crossing the dim hall. He figured out how to do this by envisioning that his companions hosted composed an unexpected gathering for him, and were holding up in the dimness.

The kid and the phantom met there, and before long, became incredible companions. So inviting did they become that the kid helped the apparition beat his dread of the light.

TRAPPED IN AQUILA'S PLACE

Aquila's place was a beautiful minimal model world in which Christianah Perfect had worked with her toys. She was continually caring for it and ensuring that everything stayed flawlessly in its place. She kept the red individuals in the red houses, the green children playing on the swings of the green parks, and the guardians talking
the entire day in the town square. It was a sweet and immaculate minimal world, and Christianah imagined that one day she might have the option to go through a day in Aquila's place.

At that point, having no clue how, her desire was satisfied, and she woke up one day in Aquila's place, all wearing pink, and made of little toy squares.

How great!

Everything was similarly as she had known it! It was extremely stunning.

Christian was totally cheerful, and after she had gotten over her astonishment, she rushed to see the swings in the green park.

Be that as it may, before she arrived, a monster hand swooped down out of the sky and grabbed her. It took her by the arm and moved her back to where she had begun from by the pink palace. Christianah was somewhat stunned by this, yet she figured out how to forget about it, since she saw her adored red houses, and off she went to investigate.

In any case, once more, the large hand descended and set her back by the pink palace.

At that point, a Princess turned out onto one of the palace galleries and addressed Christianah.

"Try not to. You will always be unable to leave the pink zone". What's more, the Princess disclosed to her how the large hand never let anybody move about in Aquila's place, and that implied that it was the saddest land in the entire world; nobody could do what they needed or go where they needed.

Christianah took a gander at the essences of all the little individuals, and she could see that it was valid. She understood that the huge hand was her own and that she had constantly utilized it to keep everything in Aquila's place consummately all together.

"So what's going on?" she inquired. "Don't all of you like living in such a beautiful, efficient land?" said Christianah.

"In the event that we can't pick what to do or where to go, what's the point?" they addressed her. "In the event that we could just have one day where we were allowed to take a brief trip and see different things... Don't you get it?"

What's more, certain, Christianah before long comprehended. Following a couple of days without having the option to choose anything for herself, nor move away from the pink palace, Christianah was feeling down; to such an extent that she never again thought about her flawless little land.

At that point, one morning, she woke again in her typical life. The primary thing she did was head toward her model world and move the little individuals going to better places.

Presently each time she discovered one strange, rather than promptly returning it, she would hang tight for a day, so the little individual would have the opportunity to appreciate the entirety of that lovely world.

Frequently, at home and at school, they had attempted to disclose to her what opportunity implied, and how significant it was. Presently there was nothing about opportunity Christianah didn't comprehend.

To thoroughly understand it, she just needed to recollect those pitiful days she had spent down in Aquila's place.

A COLLECTION OF JUNGLE ANIMALS BEDTIME STORIES FOR KIDS

JUNGLE BREW

In a little uneven village of southern India, carried on a little youngster called Bulbul. She lived in a cabin with her mom. Her home was encompassed by the tallest and greenest trees you could ever have seen. On foggy days, the leaves of plants and trees held the greatest dewdrops you could envision.

Bulbuli was as cheerful as her name. She, alongside her companions, would dance through the unlimited woodlands around her town. She wanted to take in full breaths each morning as the air conveyed a wide range of various smells. Sometimes she could smell a sweet, sweet scent. At different times it was a solid and sharp fragrance. At that point, there were days when everything she could smell was a commonplace bunch.

Awakening to those invigorating aromas was the ideal route for Bulbuli to start her day. At that point, there was Totaram, the parrot, who might fly into the town each morning, roost himself on a tree confronting Bulbuli's hovel, and advise her of the whole buzz of the woodland. He would likewise advise her of his flights to various terrains and the individuals who lived there.

Bulbuli wanted to hear Totaram's tales. She yearned to visit these terrains and see their various sights. Her heart would race and pound boisterously as Totaram would talk. However, it would consistently end with a profound murmur. She needed to quit longing for faraway terrains when she had never at any point been to Senseless Point.

Everyone in the town discussed Senseless Point. A couple of individuals from the neighboring towns had been there yet nobody from her own town. From all the discussion around, it appeared as though a secretive spot promising an encounter of a lifetime.

Bulbuli accepted that in the event that she, at any point, got the opportunity to go to Senseless Point, she would come back to her villa and depict it to everybody. She would inform everybody regarding this puzzling spot.

On this specific morning, Bulbuli sat tight for Totaram's whistle. She took care of the hens and gathered their eggs. Next, she took care of the bovines and afterward drained them. At the same time, she stopped now and again to tune in to Totaram's call. Tired of pausing, she left for her school. Every one of her understudies in her school sat under an enormous banyan tree.

Bulbuli could scarcely focus on what was being instructed.

A few days passed, and Bulbuli developed increasingly more worried about Totaram. She stressed that Totaram might be harmed. She had no chance to get to know whether he was protected. Bulbuli developed increasingly sad with every day. After school, she would stroll through the timberlands shouting to Totaram.

"Hi! Are you here someplace, Totaram?" she would shout, measuring her mouth with her hands.

At that point, one early morning, even before the sun had risen, she heard an exceptionally loud and distressed winged creature call. She jumped up and hurried out to look. It was Totaram. "Bulbuli! Wake up! I have to converse with you!"

Bulbuli loosened up her arm so that Totaram could roost on it. "Where have you been, Totaram? I have been so stressed over you. What is wrong? You appear to be exceptionally disturbed!"

"There is an inconvenience at Senseless Point. War has broken out in the backwoods."

"Quiet down, Totaram, or you will wake the whole town. What sort of difficulty would you say you are discussing? Also, who is at war?" asked a bewildered Bulbuli.

"The jungle… Oops! Sorry, Bulbuli. I do need to quit shouting. The jungles are at war. Silly Point isn't what it used to be. All the animals are alarmed. They don't have a clue what will occur straightaway. Bulbuli, we need to consider something!" cried Totaram tensely.

"I despise everything, don't comprehend. In what capacity would jungles be able to be at war? Why not take me to Senseless Point?" said Bulbuli.

Totaram became much progressively unsettled.

"Silly Point is two dawns and two nightfalls away. Your little feet won't have the option to convey you there."

"My psyche is greater than my feet, Totaram, Don't let the size of my feet fool you. I'm not reluctant to do troublesome things. Plus, the least I can do is an attempt."

"The excursion is long and hard, Bulbuli. I don't know… " pondered Totarem.

"All things considered, I can't think about some other method to help. You should take me to Senseless Point," argued Bulbuli. Totaram thought for quite a while. Hesitantly, he concurred.

"Okay, at that point, however, we should leave quickly," he said.

Simply then, Bulbuli understood that she was unable to leave without revealing to her mom. Totaram proposed that they stop while in transit to get Koyal, his companion, to reveal to her mom before anything else.

"Rush at this point. We should not lose whenever," Totaram asked.

So off they went. Totaram flew simply over Bulbuli's head and drove the way. Bulbuli strolled and strolled for a few hours. She was not unused to strolling through bushes and tall grass. Be that as it may, at that point, she became eager and tired. Totaram could see that she expected to eat and drink.

"Only somewhat longer Bulbuli. There are coconut trees ahead," said Totaram. At the point when they arrived at the coconut estates, Totaram let out an abrasive whistle. "Whoeeeee... ."

From no place swung a playful monkey. He was so loaded with beans that Totaram needed to scold him.

"Quiet down, Bandaroo! I have work for you. Quit dancing around."

"OK, Totaram. What is it?" asked Bandaroo.

"Pluck two or three coconuts and hurl them underneath. My companion Bulbuli here is eager," educated Totaram. Bandaroo obliged. He tossed down three green coconuts. They split open as they collided with the ground. Bulbuli ravenously connected for them and scooped out the smooth portion. She ate immediately when at the same time, Bandaroo screeched with charm from the tree above.

"Much obliged Bandaroo. That was filling," said Bulbuli.

"Call me anytime, people. I'm the best hurler in the jungle," said Bandaroo happily.

Totaram and Bulbuli continued with their excursion. Following a few hours, Bulbuli became tired and depleted. In any case, she was not going to surrender. She had a chance of a lifetime here. A visit to Senseless Point for individuals around her town resembled a journey.
Each time that she felt exhausted, Bulbuli attempted to picture Senseless Point in her brain. She envisioned a wonderful spot that could fill individuals' hearts with joy. That scene in her psyche was sufficient to cause her to overlook how footsore she was. The main sunset of their excursion set in.

Bulbuli was stirred by the babbling of what appeared to be a million feathered creatures in the jungle. Bulbuli took a few major breaths and extended her arms to awaken her body. The morning felt unique. She could smell all the commonplace fragrances that she used to each morning, however in some way or another, they were more grounded and additionally reviving.

"Totaram! Would you be able to smell the freshness noticeable all around? I love it!" she told the parrot. "You have the entire day to take your whiffs. Let us get going," requested Totaram.

Totaram and she talked little the following day. He could see that Bulbuli was worn out, ravenous and parched.

Totaram flew down to roost on her shoulder. "There is a stream close by. We'll rest there for some time."

In a short time, Bulbuli heard the sound of hurrying water. In the blink of an eye at all, they showed up at the stream. The unmistakable water sparkled in the daylight. The water appeared to race with itself to get someplace. It was a lovely sight.

Bulbuli hungover and measured the water in her grasp and drank all that she could. She sprinkled water all over and invigorated herself. Similarly, as she was done, Totaram arrived on her shoulder by and by and pushed her to loosen up her palms. He, at that point, dropped red, flavorful berries in them.

"Goodness, Totaram! You are the most delightful companion I know. Much thanks to you so much," grinned Bulbuli.

"Feel free to eat them. Berries are my preferred nourishment. I have just eaten an excessive number of today!" spouted Totaram.

They rested some time and afterward set out indeed. Bulbuli strolled and strolled while Totaram flew simply over her conversing with her at the same time.

Following a few hours, Bulbuli plunked down. "I have to rest, Totaram. I am actually quite depleted." Totaram let out an uproarious whistle. In no time, an elephant walked around to them. Totaram acquainted Hathi with Bulbuli and let him know of their excursion to Senseless Point.

"I accept just a human can help the war in the jungle. Animals are fleeing based on what is heaven for us," said a concerned Hathi.

"Obviously. Move up, young lady, however, I can just take you up to the path. After that, you are all alone. I can't be away from my gathering for since quite a while ago," said Hathi. Bulbuli was eased... Her little legs required rest, and she had the option to get an awesome perspective on the jungle from on Hathi's back.

Hathi, as Totaram, had numerous tales to tell. The day passed, no problem at all. At sunset, the trio settled by a cavern. Totaram and Hathi accumulated dried leaves and straw and made a bed for Bulbuli. When Bulbuli sat down, she snoozed off. At the third dawn, Totaram didn't need to wake Bulbuli.

She was up at the break of day. The little youngster, the parrot, and the elephant started the last leg of their excursion. Bulbuli was getting increasingly unsure of what's in store. First, there was the expectation of Senseless Point. At that point, there was the anxiety of the jungles at war.

As she was drawing nearer to her goal, her heart started to load up with rush and energy; however, with a tinge of dread.

In a matter of seconds, Hathi halted. I should come back to my family. All the animals would be appreciative to you on the off chance that you could help end the war of the jungles. We can't stand to live anyplace else. These jungles have been our home for ages."

Bulbuli expressed gratitude toward Hathi for conveying her to the extent he did. "I trust the jungles listen to me, Hathi.

Totaram sat on Bulbuli's shoulder and requested that her lull.

"See that trail going descending. That will lead us to Senseless Point," educated Totaram.

Now, a weird murmuring sound wrapped the jungle. As they strolled further, the commotion became stronger and stronger.

Bulbuli could scarcely accept what was happening. At no other time had she experienced such a scene. As she climbed down the path and glanced around, she didn't see anything strange. Be that as it may, the racket was ear-parting.

Totaram hamiltoned at her ear to stand out enough to be noticed. With the screeches of the jungles, Bulbuli could barely hear Totaram. Inside three additional means, Bulbuli ended up in the midst of a clearing. Maybe all the trees of the jungle had out of nowhere vanished. There were hillocks extending the extent that her eyes could see.

"This is Senseless Point. This is where everything develops wild. People scarcely ever come here," said Totaram. At that point, he started shouting, "A person is here, an individual!" But in the stunning noise of the jungles, his voice went unheard.

Bulbuli couldn't get herself to expel her hands from her ears. She was unable to comprehend what the jungles were stating, however, at this point plainly. There were three jungles included.

Out there, just before her, she could see green beds. To her right side were hundreds and many bushes with red blossoms. To her left side, she could see exceptionally tall plants. The sight before her was stunning. Furthermore, the smell was dazzling.

Bulbuli's face lit up with amazement. She turned towards every jungle a few times over, to take in the magnificence. Instantly, the clamor of the jungles started to fade away, as though the jungles had detected her.

That was when Bulbuli took her first full breath. She could smell the fragrance of Tea. At that point in the following breath, she was attracted to the scent to her right side. It was a hot scent, something she knew about. Uncertain, she took in some more and said to herself, "Ah! Elaichi!"

A delicate breeze pushed her to one side. Her head turned, and she grinned when she took in her next full breath. It was an appealing and unadulterated smell. In a flash, she perceived the plant.

Bulbuli joined her hands and bowed with adoration. "You are Tulsi!"

Bulbuli was overpowered by the scents. They possessed a scent like three octaves of a similar melodic note – Sa, Sa, Sa. Bulbuli felt upbeat. She extended her arms and whirled around with her eyes shut.

The scents and the melodic notes played in her mind, again and again. Every one of her faculties was alive. This was a supernatural minute for her. At no other time had she felt so enchanted?

Simply at that point, the Elaichi plant talked,

"Possibly, this young lady could rebuff the Tea shrubs."

"Possibly. Young lady, would you be able to prevent the Tea hedges from taking our aroma?" asked a Tulsi plant.

Bulbuli was staggered to hear the jungles address her. Before she could react, a Tea hedge made some noise. "Possibly, if these two were nowhere to be found, people may have the option to value our smell."

"Is that what this war is tied in with, stressing over your scents getting taken?" asked a confused Bulbuli. She grinned to herself. "Do you have any thought about what all of you smell like from where I stand? I can smell every one of you, unmistakably."

"It truly isn't our shortcoming. We are not aroma hoodlums. Our leaves assume the smell of whatever develops around us. Truth be told, with Tulsi and Elaichi around us, we need to strive to keep our character. It isn't as though the Tulsi jungle and the Elaichi jungle have lost their aroma to me. You recently said that you could smell their individual whiff," said a Tea shrubbery.

Bulbuli took a few full breaths to quiet down. She found that each time she took in a gathered breath of Tea, Elaichi, and Tulsi, it helped her unwind. There was something calming about them three together.

"My mom has shown me significant things from the Vedas. Do you recognize what they need to state?" asked Bulbuli. "The sun ought to be a supplier of bliss, the sky ought to be a provider of satisfaction, and all trees and plants ought to be suppliers of joy. All of these should give us true serenity. Do you think you are doing that?"

The jungles fell quiet. They were tuning in to Bulbuli. Bulbuli had a thought. She murmured something to Totaram. He took off from her shoulder very quickly.

A Tulsi plant talked. "The Elaichi and Tulsi develop wild. We have no power over where and how we develop. What's more, neither do we advise the breeze what direction to blow."

Bulbuli thought for a minute. "All things considered, how might you accuse the Tea? Perhaps you should accuse the breeze."

"The breeze! Tulsi and Elaichi battle continually with the breeze as well. They don't need the breeze to remove their aroma from here," said a Tea bramble.

Bulbuli was dismayed. "Is that valid?" she inquired.

Neither one nor the other blameworthy jungles answered. Bulbuli murmured profoundly. Simply then, Totaram returned. He conveyed a couple of Tulsi leaves, some Elaichi seeds, and Tea leaves in his mouth and put them on Bulbuli's palm. Bulbuli tenderly rubbed them together. She raised her palm to smell them. She let out a noisy pleased scream.

The jungles shouted back as one, "What is wrong, young lady?

Bulbuli giggled with delight. "You would now be able to wave the white banner for harmony. I have a touch of every one of you three in my grasp, and together, you smell like nothing else on the planet. One whiff of every one of you together is so unwinding."

Totatram murmured in Bulbuli's ear. She grinned. "Totaram reveals to me that the animals in the jungles have realized just which leaf to eat when they are unwell. Indeed, even the flying creatures have eaten your products of the soil together to know how rapidly you can improve them once more. Did you jungles even realize that?" asked Bulbuli.

"These animals eat your leaves to calm a wide range of affliction. Totaram, get me a lot of Tea, Elaichi and Tulsi. I am returning home to mix a warm cup of tea with Tulsi and Elaichi for my mom. Praise, jungles! The world is going to realize how well you taste together, which implies that you need to manage everything well with one another. Would you be able to do that?" asked Bulbuli.

Bulbuli and Totaram laughed. So did the jungles. This time the clamor level rose not in light of the battling, yet with giggling. Bulbuli was mitigated to see the war reaching a conclusion. She understood that the jungles had each had the option to feel pride in their uniqueness.

Bulbuli solicited Totaram to gather packs from Tea, Tulsi leaves alongside Elaichi seeds. "Jungles, I am currently going to come back to my town with the most wonderful and invigorating Tea, one with Tulsi and Elaichi. Also, I guarantee to come back with individuals from my town to acquaint them with Senseless Point. The most invigorating spot on earth!"

That is the means by which Tulsi and Elaichi seasoned tea was found.

THE FOOLISH DONKEY

This is a standout amongst other short story about animals with moral exercise for kids. When a lion, the lord of the timberland, was injured in a battle with an elephant. The injured lord couldn't chase for a long time and needed to stay hungry. The lion's clergyman was a shrewdness fox. Since the lion couldn't chase, the fox also needed to stay hungry.

At some point, the fox stated, "Your greatness! We both are eager, and you are as yet unfit to chase. In the event that it proceeds with like this, at that point soon, we will bite the dust!" The lion answered, "Gracious, serve! You realize that I can't pursue my injured legs. Do a certain something! Some way or another, you can figure out how to carry an animal to me. At that point, I can go without much of a stretch murder the animal, and we will both relish upon that." The fox stated, "I will attempt my best."

Saying this, the fox left from that point. On his way, he met a fat jackass. The fox's eyes twinkled. He stated, "Hi, companion! How right? I see you after quite a while. You're looking very powerless!" The jackass answered, "Yes, companion, I have become frail on the grounds that my proprietor takes a great deal of work from me and feeds me little!" The fox stated, "I truly feel sorry for your condition. Why not accompany me to the jungle! Our ruler is exceptionally kind! Our pastoral post is empty in the ruler's court." The jackass thought he was a residential animal, and he would not have the option to make due among the wild animals. The jackass was tricked by the finesse fox, and he consented to go with the fox.

The fox took him to the lion. At the point when the eager lion saw the fat jackass coming, he was unable to control himself and bounced upon the jackass. In any case, the lion missed the objective, and the frightened jackass ran from that point. Because of the lion's scramble, they lost fat prey. It made the fox very troubled. The lion was additionally pitiful to lose a decent supper. The lion mentioned the fox to attempt again and bring back the jackass.

The fox went in search of the jackass. The fox met the jackass and said in an astonishing tone, "Companion, Why did you flee this way? The lion lord was so glad to see you that he was unable to control himself and bounced up to invite you." The jackass was tricked once more. He again went with the fox to see the lion. This time, the lion was extremely cautious. At the point when the jackass arrived at very near him, the lion got him in his grasp and slaughtered him no problem at all. Both the fox and the lion were glad.

At the point when the ruler was going to eat his dinner, the fox stated, "Your grandness! I know you're eager; however, before eating, you should wash up." The ruler preferred the thought as he hadn't cleaned up for a considerable length of time. The lion continued towards the stream. At the point when the lion left that spot to scrub down, the smooth operator immediately gobbled up the cerebrum of the jackass. At the point when the lion returned and started eating, he originally gave a shot to discover the cerebrum as he was extremely enamored with it. When the cerebrum was not seen, the lion thundered and stated, "Where is the mind? Did you gobble it up?"

When the mind was not seen, the lion thundered and stated, "Where is the cerebrum? Did you gobble it up?" The fox quickly answered, "No, Your superbness! How might I set out to do this? All things considered, jackasses are without minds. In the event that he had any cerebrums, he would positively have not come here for the subsequent time!" The lion considered the point legitimate and ate his nourishment joyfully.

£   The Hare And Tortoise Story

The rabbit could run fast. I was pleased with its speed. At some point, the rabbit saw the tortoise walk gradually. The rabbit snickered at the tortoise and stated, "You are such a slowcoach!" "My dear companion! You are so glad about your speed. How about we have a race to see who is faster," the tortoise said.

Along these lines, the bunny and the tortoise had a race. The rabbit ran extremely fast and far. Sooner or later, the bunny turned around to see where the tortoise was. The tortoise was strolling gradually, and it was a long way behind the rabbit. "The tortoise will set aside an extremely long effort to draw close to me," the rabbit thought.

The rabbit began feeling exhausted. He thought to sleep. Meanwhile, he started to eat the grass. Subsequent to eating, he rested. The tortoise gradually, however, consistently passed the bunny. The rabbit abruptly woke up and saw the tortoise simply crossing the end goal.

The bunny began running fast. Be that as it may, it was past the point of no return. The tortoise previously won the race. The rabbit was amazingly disillusioned to discover his rival as of now there like a champ.

THE LEOPARD IN HIS TREE

There was at one time a panther in the jungle, and a nighttime panther he was as well. He could scarcely sleep around evening time, and, lying on the part of his superb tree, and he invested his energy watching what was going on in the timberland around evening time. This is the manner by which he came to discover that there was a criminal in that woodland. He would watch the cheat go out each night with void hands and return stacked up with his taken plunder. Sometimes the hoodlum had nabbed the senior monkey's bananas, different times he had filched the lion's wig, or squeezed the zebra's stripes. One night he even snuck home with the enormous elephant's bogus tusk, which the elephant had been covertly wearing for a long while.

Be that as it may, as the panther was a tranquil kind of feline, who inhabited the edge of everything, he would not like to express anything to anybody. He didn't consider it to be his business, and, if the truth were told, he rather appreciated finding these little privileged insights.

Thus, because of the stealthy cheat, a significant mix was being made in the realm of the animals: the elephant felt ludicrous without his bogus tusk, and the zebra currently resembled a white jackass, also the lion who, presently as uncovered as a lioness had lost all regard. A large portion of different animals was in some comparative position as well. They were angry, confounded, or absurd. However, the panther lay unobtrusively in his tree, every late evening appreciating the criminal's ventures.

In any case, one night, the cheat took some time off, and in the wake of having sat tight an extended period of time for him to show up, the panther became drained and chosen to sleep for some time. At the point when he woke up he wound up in a spot altogether different from his typical tree, he was gliding on the water of a little lake inside a cavern, and around him, he could see every one of those articles which, after quite a while after night, he had seen being taken... the cheat had chopped down his tree and taken his whole home alongside the panther himself! So the leopard, taking a bit of leeway of the cheat not being there, ran out and went directly to see different animals disclose to them where the hoodlum had shrouded every one of their things...

They all lauded the panther for having found the criminal and his fort and permitting them to recuperate their assets. At last, the animal who lost most from this was the panther, who proved unable to replant his great tree and needed to manage with a much sub-par tree situated in an extremely exhausting site... what's more, he lamented having not been worried at the issues of different animals, presently observing that over the long haul, those very issues had gotten his own.

SOPHIA THE NOSEY GIRAFFE

In Chipper Jungle, everything was serene and content until Sophia turned up. Sophia was a very tall giraffe with a long bendy neck like some elastic plant. She drove everyone insane on the grounds that she was only the nosiest and most gossipy animal anybody had ever known. What exacerbated it was that thanks to her stature and her long, bendy neck, there was no sanctum or home past her compass. There she'd be, continually putting her head in.

She watched everything and ensured everybody comprehended what was happening. This irritated such huge numbers of animals that they had a gathering and chose to show her a thing or two.

At that time, Big Bongo, the most significant of the considerable number of monkeys, chose to move to an old deserted sanctum, and he did the spot up until it was the coziest home in the entire jungle. Sophia couldn't support her interest, and one night she trod lightly over yonder and moved toward the bedroom window. The window was open, and she stuck her head inside. She was simply on time to see Big Bongo leaving the bedroom. In this way, Sophia drove her neck further in with the goal that she could tail him to the following room. It was dull inside, and she was unable to see well, indeed. However, she tailed him down a passage, and afterward into another bedroom, and afterward another...

Until finally, Sophia couldn't tail him anymore. She had come up short on the neck. Large Bongo had run all around his home, and now Sophia's neck was in one tremendous tangle.

At that point, the various animals, who were in on the stunt, approached the house to let Sophia recognize what they thought of her disturbing meddling nature. She felt so humiliated that she chose from that point on that she would utilize her long neck for more productive errands than sticking into the lives of others.

THE INVISIBLE KING OF THE JUNGLE

In the jungle of Amazon, there carried on a fly called Amazzie, and Amazzie could thunder like a lion. He found his unique capacity while still youthful, and as he grew up, he ventured out to the most distant compasses of Amazon, where nobody would know him. When he showed up, he would let tear with his freezing thunder, moving to a great extent, terrifying everybody. He would consistently utilize a similar technique, taking cover behind brambles, and letting out a compromising thunder; at that point, he would rapidly fly behind his injured individual and thunder by and by:

- "GraaAAARRR!"

Hoping to see a frightening lion, nobody saw the little fly, who rehashed his stunts time and keeping in mind that creation enjoyment of his unfortunate casualties, saying:

- "You'll never observe me. I am Leon, the fastest and most grounded animal in the jungle."

- "See? I could annihilate you with one swipe of my paw before you even acknowledged it."

- "Would you say you are apprehensive? You would be astute to be thus, for I am the most fierce lion there is."

At last, alarmed, all the animals wound up tolerating Leon, the lion as King of the Amazon jungle. Thus Amazzie began living cheerfully. He had all he needed, and when he required something, or he liked a touch of fun, he just expected to find a workable pace thundering stunts.

Be that as it may, at some point, along came Tuga, a somewhat insane tortoise. They said he had gone through years working in a carnival with the individuals, a procedure that had sent him slightly wafers. Amazzie wasn't going to botch this chance to have a fabulous time with another appearance, so he arranged his typical dread.

Be that as it may, when Tuga heard the imperceptible lion's thunders and dangers, he started murdering himself chuckling...

- "ha! A phantom lion! I once knew a phantom lion, just as an uncovered jackass and a weasel with an articulated limp... and what fun they were the point at which they moved! Please, how about we move, little lion!"

All the animals started trembling, feeling frustrated about poor Tuga. It was the first time anybody had set out to treat the horrible Leon in such a manner, and definitely, the furious lion would have no compassion for the tortoise.

Be that as it may, Amazzie couldn't chomp or hit the tortoise, his lone choice was to keep thundering and undermining. However, the insane Tuga simply continued snickering, paying no notice to the lion's enraged admonitions. Following a couple of moments unmistakably, the lion wasn't going to complete any of his dangers, and a challenging little flying creature participates with Tuga, ridiculing the lion. Amazzie took a stab at startling the little winged creature. However, it didn't work. Step by step, different animals started to participate. At long last, all the animals were snickering at the imperceptible Leon, calling him things like: "the lion that barks, however, don't nibble," "the King without any subjects" or "the ghost Lion King, the one that sits idle"...

What's more, in this way finished Amazzie's brilliant long periods of satisfaction; the fly that thundered, that compromised, that lied so a lot... to such an extent that when the time came to keep his assertion, there was no chance he could.

MANUTE THE BRAVE

"The best man in the entire clan is Manute the bold," everybody would state. You could see with your own eyes, whenever of the day, exactly how bold he was. He would hop to the ground from astonishing statures. He would battle harmful snakes, he would get scorpions with his uncovered hands- without even a recoil. They said the specific inverse about Pontoma. Nobody had seen him get even a monkey.

At some point, they stumbled over one another in the backwoods, and Manute was demonstrating Pontoma, a coral snake he had quite recently gotten when there started a storm, any semblance of which nobody had ever observed. The two of them hurried to protect themselves under some thick foliage, and there they remained until the downpour had halted.

Be that as it may, when they were going to leave the asylum, they heard the thunder of a tiger at a separation of just a few meters. The foliage was thick and thick, and the tiger wouldn't have the option to get past it to assault them. In any case, the tiger was nearly at the passage opening. On the off chance that it happened to come in and locate the two tribesmen there, they surely wouldn't get out alive. Manute was getting eager. He needed to escape that tight gap, and stand up to the tiger in open space, where he could completely utilize his incredible chasing aptitudes. Potomac was motioning at him to keep still and be peaceful, yet Manute, tired of being left with a weakling, jumped out of the brush, amazing the tiger.

The tiger endured a few profound injuries, yet before long recuperated, and hurt Manute with two swipes of its paw, tossing him to the ground. The tiger stepped up and jumped upon Manute, yet Manute's lance, in the hands of Pontoma, interfered with the tiger's assault. The tiger dismissed, injured, however, the lance moved as fast as light emission, and with mind-blowing exactness, harming the animal over and over, until it tumbled to the ground, dormant.

Manute, stunned, and draining unreservedly from his wounds, saw this while lying level on his back on the ground. At no other time had he seen anybody take on a tiger, and utilize the lance with such smoothness and quality, as he had seen Pontoma do seconds ago.

Neither of them said a thing. Manute's thankful articulation required no words to be comprehended. Nor did they need words to think about Pontoma's injured hand or the way that they were leaving a tiger skin there in the backwoods.

From that day on, individuals step by step commented less on Manute's braveness. They thought perhaps he was less bold than previously. The most unusual thing was that they currently saw that Manute's old lance was among Pontoma's things.

In any case, Manute just grinned and recalled the day he discovered that genuine courage lay not in searching out peril, however, in controlling one's dread when peril crosses your way.

THE MOCKING TIGER

The tiger was smart, fast, and solid. He was continually ridiculing different animals, especially of the weak honey bee and the moderate and cumbersome elephant.

At some point, the animals were having a gathering in a cavern when there was an avalanche that sealed up the cavern entrance. Everybody anticipated that the tiger should spare them. However, he proved unable.

At last, the honey bee got away through a modest hole between the stones.

He took off in search of the elephant, who hadn't gone to the gathering since he was feeling dismal. The elephant came and moved the stones, liberating the animals.

The animals praised both the elephant and the honey bee and were quick to be their companions. The last animal to leave the cavern was the tiger, shamefacedly. He took in his exercise, and from that the very first moment, he just observed the positive qualities in the various animals.

ICE IN THE FOREST

The square showed up in the center of the timberland one morning. It was a gigantic square of ice, as tall as a tree, as large as a hundred elephants. Likewise, it was cold to the point that nobody set out to go close. Yet, what interested the animals most was the brilliant fortune they could see inside it. The fortune looked so magnificent that the lion King himself said that whoever could get it out would be made his successor as King.

When he said this, all the animals lost their abhorrence of the cold and jumped at the square, angrily attempting to make sure about the fortune. All things considered, everybody aside from the weasel, who represented some time taking a gander at the square, viewing different animals making a colossal upheaval heaped on one another.

The elephant was utilizing his trunk as a sledge and wound up whacking the gorilla. The two later needed to go to the emergency clinic. The tiger was utilizing his hooks like a sledge drill. However, they stalled out in the ice, and when he at last figured out how to haul his paw out the paws severed. A few gazelles, understanding the square, was made of cold water, attempted to lick the straight away. Be that as it may, the outrageous cold of the water gave them a resentful stomach. The monkeys were resolved to pulverize the square, and they tossed bananas and stones at the pace of assault rifles. Be that as it may, they hit such a significant number of different animals that they needed to stop.

Thus it went on, all the animals attempting to break the square utilizing beast power, the entire day long, and without progress. At the pace, they were going and perceiving how moderate the advancement was. They understood that it would take them longer than seven days.

Nonetheless, simply then somebody stated:

- "Look! Something's moving inside the square!"

Furthermore, it was valid. It was difficult to make out, yet something was hastening about in the center of the square, directly alongside the fortune...

Was the fortune alive? Did the fortune have a proprietor living with it?

In no way like it!

It was the weasel, who before long showed up in their middle with certain bits of the fortune. They were totally dazzled to perceive how the weasel had found a workable pace without breaking the square separated. Subsequent to complimenting her, they asked her how she'd done it.

The weasel disclosed to them that before jumping at the issue, she had set aside some effort to think and watch. She presumed that the square was too huge to split it up with power, and it would take unreasonably yearn for the sun to soften it. At that point, it happened to her that she could find a good pace of the square from underneath, by burrowing a passage. Toward the finish of her passage, she fabricated a little fire, which immediately dissolved an opening in the ice above. Along these lines, with little exertion, the weasel found a workable pace!

Thus it was, that the weasel turned into the Queen of the timberland. Furthermore, she did it by indicating everybody that one can accomplish more by considering issues as opposed to by promptly taking decisive action.

THE WORLD'S RAREST CREATURE

Once, there were a few researchers in the backwoods, attempting to contemplate the rarest monster on the planet. Nobody had seen it, and its reality was just known by some remaining parts, and by its exceptional trademark call. The call was like that of a pooch with a toothache: "Oooh..wa-ooOOOH!"

Everybody needed to be the first to photo and study it. The 'monster' was a nighttime animal, so during the day, the researchers would take a break concentrating on different issues or in conversation. The most astounding of them was Sir Walter Tick-Fondler. He was an extremely wonderful and solid chap, with a modest little mustache and an immense wayfarer's cap. Consistently, before tea, he would go through an hour sitting at his work area, placing all his gear and odds and ends in their legitimate spot. He did this with careful exactness. The scratchpad went directly at the most distant edge of the work area, on the correct hand side, marginally past the recorder, and beside the five pencils, which were consistently in a similar request: dark, red, blue, green and yellow. The light was consistently towards the finish of the work area, by the camera, on the left... thus it was with every one of his things, even with the littlest of subtleties.

Everybody was delighted that this courteous fellow was such an ideal case of the acclaimed English fixation on hand.

The researchers spent numerous evenings around there before the animal showed up, and before it did so, some of them even questioned its reality. It showed up out of nowhere, while everything hushed up.

Just a couple of meters away, the researchers heard its call noisy and clear. The well-known call of the pooch with a toothache. It kept going just a moment, since all the uproar of the researchers scrabbling for their cameras and journals terrified the animal, and it shot off before it could evidently be seen or considered in any detail.

The following morning they all analyzed their discoveries. Some had figured out how to record its call, others had noted down how it moved, and the most blessed of all had even figured out how to photo parts of its tail or legs. They all complimented each other on what they had got, however when they saw what Sir Walter had, they were stunned.

He had taken a few complete photographs, just as recording its cry, and making full-shading explanations on the animal!

Also, they were all ideal!

They raced to salute him as the best researcher of all. They currently comprehended that his fixation on request had been simply an ideal approach to get ready for working in obscurity. This had implied Sir Walter had no issue in finding and utilizing the recorder, the camera, the scratchpad, and the pencils, all in just portions of a second and without searching for them.

Obviously, the work he did on 'The Rarest Creature in the World' put Sir Walter on the map. He established an effective school for researchers and researchers called IOTO: 'So as To Investigate,' and had the pleasure of naming the animal. Furthermore, as it had all been such enjoyment and he so delighted in the field trip, in the wake of recording that trademark call, he didn't stop for a second to name the animal the 'Whatahoot.'

A COLLECTION OF ANIMALS BEDTIME STORIES FOR KIDS

JOSH HAMILTON, TIGHTROPE WADDLER

Josh Hamilton was a homestead duck whose huge dream was to turn into a tightrope walker.

Consistently he went through hours out on the rope, rehearsing, supported by his dedicated companion, Artie Quack. Artie was a more seasoned duck who, when youthful, had drilled that exact same craftsmanship. Them two were a piece fold footed at it. However, they had never let that hinder doing everything they could to continue preparing and ideally improve.

At some point, another slam showed up at the ranch. Not long after seeing the ducks' tightrope practice, he came over and started commending them. He said they were doing incredible, and he wagers they could cross any slope on that rope of theirs. This left Josh feeling profoundly empowered, in spite of Artie remarking that he hadn't seen any genuine improvement.

A couple of days after the fact, Josh ended up with the slam, looking over a gorge.

The hole was wide to the point that nobody could bounce it. You could just cross it utilizing a tightrope. Artie attempted to work his companion out of it. He needed him to understand that he wasn't such an extraordinary tightrope walker, and this thing with the gorge would be extremely hazardous. The smash deviated, guaranteeing them that Josh Hamilton was the best tightrope walker in the entire district and that Artie Quack was only envious of him. The two ducks blew up, and Artie wouldn't help with the tightrope walk.

On the gorge, the slam egged Josh on, to arrive at the opposite side. In any case, when he had ventured out onto the rope, Josh lost his parity and fell. Luckily he arrived on a little edge, yet when he requested that the smash help him up, he found that he had vanished. Josh Hamiltons needed to invest very some energy there, and surprisingly more terrible, his leg was broken.

He understood that his old companion Artie had been coming clean with him from the start. He saw that it couldn't have been simple for Artie to reveal to him that he was anything but a decent tightrope walker, and Josh was thankful to have such an old buddy who might consistently come clean with him...

Also, Artie truly was an old buddy, since, recognizing what was going to occur, he had gone straight off to discover a gathering of wild ducks - old companions of his. These wild ducks flew obviously superior to the poor old ranch ducks. Artie arranged a salvage activity with the wild ducks.

Josh asked Artie to pardon him, and Artie joyfully did as such. Furthermore, while being protected and flying high, Josh could see that over on the opposite side of the gorge, there was a heap of all-around covered up and scrumptious indulgences. Josh understood that that was all the ravenous smash had been keen on. He needed those nourishments, yet couldn't cross the gorge himself, so he had attempted to utilize Josh to get them.

Josh felt silly, yet in addition, blessed, on the grounds that helped by his new duck companions, they figured out how to assemble such awesome nourishment, take it to the ranch, and host a major gathering among genuine companions.

HUMILITY AMONG THE ANIMALS

There was, at one time, a kangaroo who turned into the champion of a game. Nonetheless, with this achievement, he got pompous and terrible, and he invested a great deal of energy ridiculing others.

His preferred objective was a little penguin whose walk was so moderate and cumbersome that it regularly kept him from completing the race.

One day the fox, who sorted out the races, let everybody realize that his most loved for the following race was the poor penguin. Everybody thought it was a joke, yet at the same time, the huge headed kangaroo got irate, and he disparaged the penguin considerably more than expected. The penguin would not like to partake in the race. However, it was a custom that everybody must do as such. Upon the arrival of the race, he moved toward the beginning line in a gathering which was following the fox. The fox drove them up the mountain, while everybody ridiculed the penguin, remarking on whether he would move down the mountain or simply slide down on his fat tummy.

Be that as it may, when they arrived at the top, they all shut up. The highest point of the mountain ended up being a hole that had loaded up with water, making it into a lake. Now, the fox gave the beginning sign, saying: "First to the opposite side successes."

The penguin, energized, waddled awkwardly to the water's edge. When he was in the water, however, his speed was top-notch, and he won the race by a long separation. In the meantime, the kangaroo scarcely figured out how to arrive at the opposite side; sad, mortified, and half suffocated. If it appeared as though the penguin was standing by to ridicule the kangaroo, the penguin had taken in a great deal from his misery, and as opposed to disparaging the kangaroo, he offered to show him how to swim.

For the remainder of the day, the animals had a good time playing in the lake. However, the person who had fun the most was the fox, who, with his astuteness, had figured out how to cut the kangaroo down a peg or two.

THE BEAUTY CONTEST

Once, in a dazzling nursery, experienced the most lovely butterfly on the planet. She was so beautiful and had won such a significant number of magnificence challenges that she had gotten vain. To such an extent, that one day, the brassy cockroach got tired of her flaunting and chose to show her a thing or two.

She went to see the butterfly, and before everybody, she revealed to her that she wasn't generally that wonderful and that if the butterfly won challenges, it was on the grounds that the jury had been bribed. In all actuality, the cockroach was the most delightful.

The butterfly was enraged, and with chuckling and scorn told the cockroach, "I'll beat you in a delight challenge, with whichever jury you yourself pick."

"Alright, I acknowledge. See you on Saturday," addressed the cockroach without hanging tight for an answer.

That Saturday, everybody went to the excellence challenge, the butterfly showing up totally sure of triumphboard: cockroaches, worms, bugs, and nits. The entirety of the adjudicators favored the dreadful crawlies and terrible stench of the cockroach, which effectively won the challenge.

The butterfly was left crying and embarrassed, needing never to participate in another magnificent challenge in her life. Luckily, the cockroach pardoned the butterfly for her vanity, and they became companions. Sometime later, the butterfly even won the Humility Contest.

THE BRAVE LITTLE TORTOISE AND THE MONSTER

Quite a long time ago, there was a tortoise on a boat, and the boat sank. Sometime later, the tortoise made it to a desert land encompassed by water on all sides aside from one. The landward side hinted at a major, steep, jagged mountain. To abstain from starving to death, the tortoise chose to move to the highest point of the mountain, trusting that he would have the option to cross to the opposite side.

At the point when he found a workable pace secured summit, he was freezing cold, and afterward, a snowstorm began. He just figured out how to make out a little pathway driving down the opposite side of the mountain. In any case, the way was monitored by a major beast that wouldn't quit yelling.

"Uuh!"

Such a sight and sound nearly murdered the tortoise with dread, and all he needed to do was conceal his head inside his shell. In any case, checking out him, he saw that numerous different animals were lying solidified to death, and with looks of frightfulness on their countenances. So the tortoise didn't go into his shell.

He called up the entirety of his mental fortitude to descend the way towards the beast. The closer the tortoise got, the more the beast changed its shape. At that point, when he was nearly upon it, the tortoise understood that what he had thought was a beast, was just an incredible heap of rocks, which framed a shape simply like a beast. Concerning the "uuh," the tortoise understood this was only the sound of the breeze blowing through a little cavern.

The tortoise continued, and in the long run, slid into a wonderful valley, loaded up with woods, and a lot of nourishment. The tortoise lived cheerfully here and became referred to wherever as the Brave Little Tortoise.

THE LITTLE WORM IS LOST

There was, at one time, a little worm that lived in an apple in a tree alongside a house where a few children lived.

At some point, however, the worm didn't wave back, and the toys, stressed, began yelling for him. They searched for him all over, yet discovered nothing. The toys continued looking until they heard a weird clamor originating from the carport. They ran over and discovered only some more toys. Be that as it may, when they were all calm, they could at present hear the clamor, and it drove them to a football.

Everybody began yelling for the worm once more, and from inside, the ball seemed a little head, saying: "alright, fine, yet I'm sleeping. Wouldn't anyone be able to have any harmony in their home any longer?" They all chuckled, and afterward, the worm comprehended that he was no longer in his apple.

In the midst of his shocked articulations, and his companions addressing, in strolled a wanderer feline and stated,

- "I saw everything; I can mention to you what occurred."

Thus the feline disclosed to them that the earlier night the little worm had been out on the town, living it up. At the point when he came back to the tree, it was at that point dim, and he was unable to see his apple. He had wound up sleeping inside the football, which the children had before kicked into the tree's limbs. Also, the following morning, before leaving, the children's dad had gathered the ball.

They all appreciated finding out about the experience and were happy nothing terrible had happened to the little worm. In any case, while the worm was coming back to his tree, somewhat irritated by the toys' giggling, he pondered internally that he would need to be more mindful so as to return home before dull...

THE DUCK RACE

Speedy and Quack were two valiant, energetic little ducks who lived with their mom. Both were truly fast and were continually contending with one another. They dashed each other in numerous types of places. Ashore, sea and air; running, swimming, or flying.

At some point, subsequent to visiting their Uncle Ducklass upriver, Quick yelled, "last one home is a goose!" and the two ducks swam rapidly downriver. The two of them knew the way well.

However, Quack had been setting up a stunt for quite a while. He had understood that the ebb and flow in the stream was more grounded, and would support him. Thus, despite the fact that Mother Duck had let them know never to swim in the stream, Quack rowed over to it. "I'm mature enough currently to swim here," he pondered internally.

It wasn't well before he understood his mom had been correct. He was going a lot faster than Quick and was building up a major lead. Snappy was not entertained. He never resisted his mom, and now his obedience implied he would lose the race! As they went on, the current got more grounded.

Quack triumphantly crossed the end goal, without acknowledging he was set out directly toward a major whirlpool in the stream. Before he could respond, there he was turning around in it, unfit to getaway.

Getting him out of there was no simple issue. No duck was sufficiently able to swim in those waters, and poor Quack continued gulping water. The way that his head was turning like a top didn't improve the situation much either.

Luckily, a cow from a close-by ranch stopped by and, seeing Quack, swam in and saved him, to keep him from drinking all the water in the waterway. At the point when he was on dry ground, he stayed unsteady for a long while. That gave a significant snicker to the various different animals that had been viewing.

That day, Quick comprehended that he had done well to tune in to his mom, despite the fact that from the outset, it may have appeared the troublesome alternative. With respect to Quack... well... Quack couldn't overlook that experience, despite the fact that he needed to. From that point on, at whatever point he contacted a drop of water, he tumbled to the floor and spun cycle three times before having the option to find a good pace.

Blustery days demonstrated very engagingly

THE NATURAL GARDEN

There was previously a King who had an incredible palace with superb nurseries. In those nurseries, there lived a huge number of animals from several distinct species. They were of extraordinary assortment and shading, and they transformed that place into a sort of heaven that everybody could appreciate.

There was just a single thing in those nurseries that the King detested: close to the inside stood the remaining parts of what had been, hundreds of years back, an enormous tree, yet that presently was shriveled and dry, and cheapened the shading and excellence of its environment. This pestered the King so much that he, at long last, arranged it to be chopped down and supplanted by a delightful arrangement of wellsprings.

Sometime later, a shrewd honorable was visiting the King at his palace. He murmured in the King's ear:

- "Greatness, you are the most shrewd of men. Wherever one hears discussion of the magnificence of these nurseries and the huge number of animals that populate them. Be that as it may, during the time I've spent here, I've scarcely observed something besides this wellspring and only a couple of little fowls… What trickery!"

The King, who never attempted to hoodwink anybody, found, regrettably, that what the honorable had revealed to him was valid. They had spent such huge numbers of months appreciating the wellsprings that they hadn't understood that scarcely any animals stayed in the nurseries. Without sitting around idly, he sent for the court's specialists and counselors. The King needed to tune in to numerous untruths, creations, and suspicions, yet nothing could clarify what had occurred. Not in any case, the extraordinary prize offered by the King figured out how to recover the illustrious nurseries' previous quality.

Numerous years after the fact, a youngster introduced himself to the King, guaranteeing him that he could clarify what had occurred, and how the animals could be returned.

- "What occurred with your nursery is that there sufficiently wasn't crap, your grandness. Especially moth crap."

Every one of those present chuckled at the youngster's joke. The gatekeepers prepared to toss him out. However, the King halted them.

- "I need to hear what you need to state. From the thousand untruths I've heard, none have started that way."

The youngster proceeded, intense, and began clarifying how the nurseries' huge animals took care of for the most part on the little splendidly hued winged creatures, who owed their appearance to their own nourishment, made out of brilliant worms, who thusly benefited from different uncommon types of plants and blossoms that could just developed in that piece of the World, just insofar as there was sufficient moth crap for them... thus he kept, telling how the moths were the premise of a lot of nourishment for some different winged creatures, whose crap supported the presence of new types of plants that took care of different creepy crawlies and animals, and which were, thusly, crucial to the presence of different species... Also, the youngster would have continued talking immediately if the King had not yelled.

- "Enough! What's more, would you be able to reveal to me how you know every one of these things, being so youthful?"

Asked the King.

- "Well, since now, all from your nursery are at my home. Before I was brought into the world, my dad gathered that old tree you had removed from the center of the nursery, and he planted it in our nursery. From that point forward, each spring, from out of that tree come a large number of moths. With time, the moths pulled in the winged creatures, and new plants and trees developed, giving nourishment to different animals that, thusly, gave nourishment to other people... And now, my dad's old spot is loaded up with life and shading. All gratitude to the moths from the enormous old tree."

- "Brilliant!"

shouted the King,

- "Presently, I'll have the option to recuperate my nurseries. What's more, you, I'll make you rich. Have confidence that inside seven days, everything will be prepared. Use the same number of men as you like."

- "Your Majesty, I'm worried about the possibility that that can't be,"

said the youngster,

- "In the event that you like, I can attempt to reproduce the nurseries, yet you won't live to see it. It will take numerous years for the regular parity to restore itself. With extraordinary favorable luck, maybe I, when I'm old, will see it finished. Things like these don't rely upon what number of men deal with them."

The essence of the old King was miserable and thoughtful, seeing how fragile was the parity of nature, and how reckless it had been to break it so cheerfully. In any case, he so cherished those nurseries and those animals that he chose to fabricate a gigantic palace beside the youngster's property. What's more, with a large number of men taking a shot at the development, he figured out how to see the palace completed in substantially less time than would have been important to restore the parity of nature of that garden in some other spot.

THE SINGING HIPPO

Sometime in the distant past, a hippopotamus lived in a stream alongside a major and lone tree.

At some point, a fowl came and settled in the tree. The melodies and the trip of the winged creature caused such jealousy in the hippo that he was unable to consider whatever else. Consistently he would regret the way that he had been brought into the world a hippo. This, in spite of the multiple occasions the feathered creature told the hippo he was so fortunate to be so large and such a decent swimmer.

At long last, the hippo made his brain up that he would leave the waterway, climb the tree, go out to roost on a branch, and begin singing. In any case, when he attempted to climb the tree, it was very certain that the hippo didn't have wings nor paws to move with, and neither might he be able to jump.

Understanding that he could never oversee it, he furiously slammed his entire load against the tree until it came colliding with the ground. At that point, triumphantly, he ventured onto the leaves of the fallen tree and started singing.

Lamentably, hippos can't sing either. All that originated from his mouth were loathsome clamors, and when different animals heard this, they all assembled round to ridicule the hippo remaining on the part of a fallen tree, attempting to sing like a flying creature.

He was so humiliated by this that he chose to never again lament being a hippo. He additionally felt awful about having thumped the tree over. He utilized his entire existence to raise the tree back up once more, replant it, and care for it until it had totally recuperated.

DARK WIZARD, SPARK WIZARD

At whatever point there was a tempest, the animals of the Enchanted Forest ran, scared, to hide, fearful of the electrical discharges and the frightening thunder. Nonetheless, one day the tempest went ahead so rapidly that practically nobody had the opportunity to arrive at their alcove and, exactly when they were generally alarmed, a portion of the animals saw a minor minimal light show up from out of the trees, originating from a spot where an electrical discharge had quite recently hit.

The little light was hopping and cheerfully and energetically shouting out. All the animals viewing went to see who this distraught being could be. A being would be glad in a tempest.

Thus it was that they met the absolute first of the Spark Wizards, which were minor little creatures that shone strongly all finished, as though they had some way or another figured out how to swallow a star. Stone, as this Spark Wizard was known, ended up being decent and extremely enchanting, he answered with shock:

- "Yet, is there any valid reason why I wouldn't be cheerful when I've quite recently gotten away following 2,000 years?"

He proceeded to clarify how, a large number of years back, the Dark Wizard had caught all the Spark Wizards and detained them inside some huge dark mists where he constrained them to fill in as his slaves. It was practically difficult to get away from that jail, however, every so often, a portion of those mists would impact, and with that sway little tufts of cloud would sever, permitting a Spark Wizard to getaway. Each time one got away from, it would jump out with such energy that its path of light would enlighten the entire sky, and produce what we know as a lightning jolt. Not long after such a getaway, the Dark Wizard would acknowledge what had occurred and would protest angrily about it and beat the mists in dissatisfaction. His cries were loaded up with outrage, and this is the reason moves of thunder blast so emphatically around the skies.

Energized at Flint's story, those animals were never again alarmed at the tempests and the thunder. Rather, when the sky started to cover with dark mists, all the animals would assemble at the enormous stone, where they could get the best perspective on the tempest. There they would praise and cheer each time a little Spark Wizard figured out how to get away from the grip of the Dark Wizard. Surprisingly better, each time the Dark Wizard turned out with one of his furious protests of dissent, the animals would answer him with a tune of boos and sneers.

CPSIA information can be obtained
at www.ICGtesting.com
Printed in the USA
BVHW062256030521
606332BV00008B/1586